MODERN
FILM
SCRIPTS

A MAN AND A WOMAN

a film by

Claude Lelouch

English translation and description of action
by Nicholas Fry

Lorrimer Publishing, London

General Editor: Sandra Wake

SBN Cloth 0 900855 72 X
SBN Paper   900855 71 I

CONTENTS

A NOTE ON THIS EDITION

Claude Lelouch never writes a shooting script. As he is himself both director and chief cameraman, he improvises almost every scene as he goes along. The original French version of this script, published by *l'Avant-Scène du Cinéma*, was therefore built up from a shot-by-shot viewing of the film. This version was then translated into English and carefully checked and revised against a print of the film obtained from the English distributor, in order to make it as accurate a representation as possible of the film which the English or American spectator will see on the screen.

It should be pointed out that in only two or three of the so-called tracking shots was the camera mounted on a truck. In all other cases the effect was obtained either by Lelouch himself walking with the camera or else, as noted when it occurs, by a zoom.

Acknowledgments are due to *l'Avant-Scène du Cinéma* for providing stills, and to United Artists for supplying a print of the film.

THE DIRECTOR AS MATADOR

A Man and A Woman was my sixth full-length film, but also, in a way, the first, as it was for Trintignant and Anouk Aimée.

The subject? Passion against marriage, life against death, speed against love. It was a film of emotions. The sound was more important than the words, the colours more enchanting than the scenery. Every moment was a cry, the sound of a car engine, a song. It was, I think, my first romantic film. With this film I became convinced that one must not narrate but express. What the characters did not say was often more important than what they said.

It could be seen as the classic situation: a film with three characters — the husband, the wife, the lover. But with the husband dead from the beginning of the very first shot the three main characters are in fact the past, the present and the future. From the moment Jean-Louis Trintignant meets, at the Gare Saint Lazare, the woman whom he left two hours earlier at Deauville, the past and the present no longer count for me — Anne and Jean-Louis are already in the future.

. . . The most important things in life happen in hundredths of a second. At those moments one doesn't have time to set up a film unit, arrange a set and a camera and give directions. No, one has got to record life in its hundredths of a second, to shoot quickly and as much as possible. . . .

Sometimes one is a tenth of a second too late in filming, and then one has to re-create the event. That is why I give my actors information about the psychology of the characters whom they represent, but I never advise them about the mechanics of the characterisation. What is the point of marking out the exact place where an actor must stop with a piece of chalk? If he is thinking of his mark he is no longer alive.

One of the key scenes in the film, for instance, is the meeting between Jean-Louis and Anne on the beach. Jean-Louis has just come back from the Monte Carlo Rally. He has driven 6,000 kilometres to see the woman he loves. Neither Anouk

11

nor Jean-Louis had rehearsed the scene, they neither of them knew where or at what moment they were going to kiss for the first time in their lives. In view of the 6,000 kilometres Jean-Louis had travelled for that kiss, one really couldn't say to the actor : ' Sorry, old man, you kissed her a metre too far on.' The director has got to be everywhere at once. I had cleared the field of view through 360 degrees; my assistants were posted in a circle two kilometres away to prevent anyone from getting through. So when Jean-Louis came running towards Anouk I was right there with them, I was facing Jean-Louis, with Anouk, far away from her, ten centimetres away from her, beside the couple and a hundred metres away at the same time.

In this case the director can be compared to a matador — the camera is the bullfighter's cape, and each shot a thrust of his sword. He must continually provoke the actor and watch him, but with the same mixture of freedom and compulsion with which the matador plays the bull.

I am convinced that the director will in the future be an inciter, a demiurge, a creator in his own right. Directing a film is not a matter of establishing fixed positions; it is creating an impetus, giving movement to a mechanism. It is the first move which counts. God (if he exists) is a great director; he gave the world its initial impetus and now the world carries on without him; life in the world is a long film sequence in which the hand of God can no longer even be felt. His discretion is admirable — we no longer feel the presence of God behind the beauty of a sunset. That's what great directing is.

. . . Parallel worlds, space, time, series of events, probability — *A Man and A Woman* was a film which encompassed all these themes. My characters were placed in a precise temporal context (from the 1st to the 22nd January), in a defined spatial area (Deauville, Paris, Monte Carlo), and also moved in parallel worlds. (In the car with Jean-Louis, Anouk remembers an identical scene she experienced with her husband at Saintes-Maries-de-la-Mer, some years before). Then, finally, the question of probability : for a year Anouk and Jean-Louis have been going to Deauville each Sunday. They have never met. It is inevitable that one Sunday evening Anouk should miss her train. . . .

This question of probability also operated on the level of the actors themselves. I often told Anouk the opposite to what I wanted from her. At the same time I gave Trintignant or Barouh the wrong words. During the shooting, the actors would surprise each other and react in totally unexpected ways; they would expose themselves psychologically. Basically, directing is nothing more than a process of exposure — of a set, a script, the actors, the world. . . .

CLAUDE LELOUCH in conversation
with PIERRE UYTTERHOEVEN

CREDITS:

Scenario and dialogue by	Claude Lelouch in collaboration with Pierre Uytterhoeven
Directed by	Claude Lelouch
Production company	Les Films 13 (Paris)
Music composed by	Francis Lai
Lyrics by	Pierre Barouh
Arrangements by	Ivan Julien and Maurice Vander
Music for ' Samba Saravah ' composed by	Baden Powel
Original words by	Vinicius de Moraes
Adapted by	Pierre Barouh
Songs sung by	Nicole Croisille Jean-Claude Briodin Pierre Barouh
Director of photography	Claude Lelouch
Lighting cameramen	Patrice Pouget and Jean Collomb
Assistant director	Claude Gorsky
Assistant cameraman	Daniel Lacambre
Sound engineers	Michel Fano and Jean Baronnet
Assistant editor	Claude Barrois
Student editor	Marie-Claude Poyer
Art director	Robert Luchaire
Explosions	Jean Belieu
Production director	Roger Fleytoux
Administrator	Pierre Pardon
Hairstyles by	Denise Lemoigne and Jacques Cousty
Costumes by	Richard Marvil
Processing by	Eclair
Process	Eastmancolour
Length	4,068 metres
Running time	147 minutes
First shown	Cannes Film Festival, 1966

14

Distributed in Great Britain
and the United States of
America by   United Artists

Prizes : Grand Prix du XXe Anniversaire du Festival Inter-
national du Film (Cannes 1966)
Grand Prix de l'Office Catholique International du
Cinéma (Cannes 1966)
Grand Prix de la Commission Supérieure Technique
du Cinéma (Cannes 1966)

CAST:

Anne Gauthier	Anouk Aimée
Jean-Louis Duroc	Jean-Louis Trintignant
Pierre Gauthier	Pierre Barouh
Valerie Duroc	Valerie Lagrange
Antoine Duroc	Antoine Sire
Françoise Gauthier	Souad Amidou
The Headmistress	Simone Paris
Yane, Jean-Louis' mistress	Yane Barry
Jean-Louis' co-driver	Henri Chemin
Radio Commentator	Gérard Sire
The Pump Attendant	Paul le Person

A MAN AND A WOMAN

Black screen, then details of the prizes won by the film at the 1966 Cannes Film Festival (see credits) come up in white letters on colour film. No sound.

1. Long shot of a grey wintry sky. Pan right to medium close-up of a woman of about thirty, ANNE GAUTHIER, *well wrapped up in a brown, fur-trimmed coat. She keeps brushing back a lock of hair as the wind off the sea blows it across her face. As she speaks she looks down at someone out of frame. Behind her are a jetty and a lighthouse and the grey-green sea stretching away into the mist. Foghorns sound across the water against the cries of seabirds.*

ANNE : . . . So then the little girl started to undress and got into her grandmother's bed . . . and her grandmother . . . the little girl was very curious you see . . . because her grandmother looked rather funny. . . . So the little girl said to her : ' Oh grandmother, what big eyes you've got ! ' And then her grandmother said to her : ' All the better to see you with my dear.' — ' Oh grandmother, what a long nose you've got ! ' — ' All the better to smell you with my dear.' — ' Oh grandmother, what big teeth you've got ! '

As she says these words ANNE *spreads her arms and crouches down. Zoom backwards as she hugs and kisses her daughter,* FRANÇOISE, *who is also well wrapped up in a scarf and a woollen hat. (Production still on page 1)*

ANNE : ' All the better to eat you with my dear.' . . . And . . . *laughing* . . . she ate her up. . . . *A pause.* Well, did you like my story ?

FRANÇOISE : No. . . .

2. Long shot of the sea: a red fishing boat comes out of the mist towards us, turns and moves along beside the jetty, camera moving with it. FRANÇOISE *and* ANNE *continue talking off-screen.*

16

Anne *off* : No? Why not?
Françoise *off* : It's too sad.
Anne *off* : Oh! What do you want me to tell you instead then?
Françoise *off* : 'Bluebeard'.
Anne *off* : 'Bluebeard'? . . . Wait a moment. . . . 'Bluebeard' . . . Ah yes: Once upon a time . . . *Loud music as the fishing boat moves away.*

3. Medium shot of Anne *and her daughter, hand in hand, walking away from camera across a wooden footbridge, which appears foreshortened as the scene is shot through a telephoto lens. They pass several fishermen watching their lines. Although we do not hear her voice,* Anne *is clearly telling the story of Bluebeard, gesturing as she walks. The first part of the credits comes up, consisting of the title and the names of the actors.*

4. Long shot of a road with a sign-post which says: Deauville — Winter Casino. *The sky is less cloudy than in the previous scene, with patches of bright blue. A man of about thirty,* Jean-Louis Duroc, *comes towards us. He is wearing dark glasses and an overcoat and has a cigar clenched between his teeth. Camera pans as he comes across and stops beside a parked car, the windscreen of which is partly visible in a corner of the frame. The music ends. Acting very cool,* Jean-Louis *snaps his fingers at the chauffeur, who is not seen. Cries of seabirds, off.*

Jean-Louis : Antoine!
Still standing by the car, he takes the dashboard cigar-lighter from the chauffeur, who is still not seen.
Jean-Louis : Lower the top, please.
The convertible top starts to open automatically, partly visible to one side of the screen, while Jean-Louis *lights his cigar, then leans over to put the lighter back in the dashboard. Pan briefly to follow this movement. The camera is in front of the car, facing the windscreen, the chauffeur still out of frame. Finally* Jean-Louis *gets into the passenger seat, seen through the windscreen, opens a copy of 'Time' magazine and starts to leaf through it,*

17

addressing the chauffeur as he does so.

JEAN-LOUIS : To the golf course. . . .

5. *A closer shot of* JEAN-LOUIS *through the windscreen. The car is now moving, apparently swerving slightly from side to side, camera tracking out in front of it.*

JEAN-LOUIS : . . . No . . . to the go-karts !

6. *Medium close-up of* JEAN-LOUIS.

JEAN-LOUIS : No, to the harbour ! . . .

7. *Close-up of* JEAN-LOUIS *(as 5). He lowers his magazine.*

JEAN-LOUIS *his cigar clenched in his teeth* : No, to the golf course ! . . . *A pause.*

8. *Medium close-up again (as 6).*

JEAN-LOUIS : Antoine, on second thoughts, let's go to the go-karts.

9. *Resume on close-up of* JEAN-LOUIS. *The car continues to move. Camera moves to the right as* JEAN-LOUIS *suddenly throws aside his magazine and grabs the steering wheel. Zoom backwards to reveal the chauffeur, who is none other than* JEAN-LOUIS' *son,* ANTOINE, *about five or six years old. Cries of seabirds, off. In grabbing hold of the wheel, his father has apparently dropped some cigar ash on his hand.*

ANTOINE : Oh ! . . . that hurt.

JEAN-LOUIS *straightening the wheel* : Oh ! Did I hurt you. . . . Oh ! I'm sorry . . . I didn't mean to hurt you ! . . . *Full of concern.* Did I hurt you taking your hands off the wheel ?

JEAN-LOUIS *takes the cigar from his mouth and steers the car with his arms round his son. We can now see that it is a red Ford Mustang convertible.*

ANTOINE : Yes.

JEAN-LOUIS : I beg your pardon, Antoine.

10. *Long shot of the sea front at Deauville; on the right is the sea, on the left a row of beach huts on a wooden promenade. Theme music in. The camera tracks forward as the rest of the credits come up, giving the names of the production team.*

11. *Close-up through the windscreen of the Mustang.*

18

The child is still in the driving seat, wearing his father's
sunglasses which are far too large for him. JEAN-LOUIS
has his arms round him, holding the steering wheel. (Still
on page 2) Camera pans to JEAN-LOUIS, *smiling.*
12. Medium shot of the two of them, still seen through
the windscreen. JEAN-LOUIS *undoes his scarf and lifts the*
sunglasses which have slipped down over ANTOINE'S *nose.*
They both laugh.
13. The theme music continues. Long shot of ANNE *and*
FRANÇOISE *in a busy shopping street. Women hurry past*
as the two of them look in a shop window.
ANNE : Oh . . . You've lost weight. Why have you lost
weight?
FRANÇOISE : Don't know.
ANNE : Don't you eat enough at school? . . . Don't you like
the food?
14. Medium shot: camera tracks out in front of them as
they walk along.
ANNE : Would you like a piece of chocolate?
They stop in front of a grocer's. The music stops.
FRANÇOISE : No, I want a cake.
ANNE : A cake? Well, I don't know if there's a baker's here.
What kind of cake do you want?
Zoom back as they walk past the grocer's display on
the pavement. ANNE *knocks down a board with a price*
written on it. She bends down and picks it up.
ANNE : Oh! . . . Look what I've done. FRANÇOISE *laughs.*
Isn't that funny? *They both laugh.*
15. Music in again. Medium close-up of JEAN-LOUIS *and*
ANTOINE, *facing us, driving down a street in the Mustang.*
They look up, laughing, as the automatic top closes. We
hear the whine of its motor.
16. Medium long shot of another street. ANNE *and*
FRANÇOISE *have stopped in front of a shoe shop.*
ANNE : Aren't they pretty?
FRANÇOISE : Yes.
ANNE : Would you like a pair of little boots like that?
FRANÇOISE : No. I want a cake.
ANNE : All right, so you want a cake.

19

17. Medium shot of Jean-Louis *driving the Mustang along the beach. Camera tracks sideways with the car, the breaking waves in the background.*
18. Long shot of the Mustang, through yellow ochre filter. Camera pans to and fro as it turns, brakes, accelerates, turns again, rear wheels sliding across the sand. (Still on page 2) Cries of seabirds, and joyous laughter from Antoine.
19. Another similar shot. Antoine, *beaming with joy, is sitting on his father's knee as* Jean-Louis *continues to hurl the car from side to side.*
20. Long shot in normal colour, then zoom in on the car again as it brakes, then accelerates.
21. Finally the third and last part of the credits (the sound team and director) comes up against a long shot of trees seen across the water, lit by the last rays of the setting sun. Camera tracks sideways past several fishing boats, silhouetted against the water.

22. Long shot of the grounds of the private school attended by Françoise *and* Antoine, *in Deauville. It is evening, and the scene is shot in black and white through a blue filter. Children run past the camera towards a flight of steps leading up to the main entrance. Pan left as* Anne, *carrying a couple of parcels, and* Françoise *both hurry towards the steps.*
Anne *to* Françoise : Hurry up . . . quick . . . I'll miss my train . . . hurry . . .
They stop at the bottom of the steps. Anne *bends down to kiss her daughter and give her the parcels.*
Anne : See you next Sunday, darling. . . . Don't catch cold. . . . Hurry inside.
She gives a final wave of the hand and Françoise *goes up the steps and in through the door. Camera pans as* Anne *hurries away.*
23. Low angle medium shot of the Headmistress, *a well-preserved blonde woman, as she accompanies another mother down the steps to a chauffeur-driven Bentley which is waiting at the bottom. Camera pans right with*

20

them.

HEADMISTRESS : Goodbye. . . .

Several children run past camera. The Bentley turns in the driveway and moves off, and we see the headlamps of the Mustang approaching. Pan left as it comes to a halt in front of the steps. The HEADMISTRESS, *who is wearing an overcoat and scarf, addresses* JEAN-LOUIS *with mock severity.*

HEADMISTRESS : A fine thing I must say . . . driving with the hood down in the middle of December.

JEAN-LOUIS : It's not me, it's Antoine.

HEADMISTRESS : That's right . . . blame it on Antoine.

JEAN-LOUIS : Come on Antoine.

As he speaks, JEAN-LOUIS *gets out of the car, walks round it and goes up the steps with* ANTOINE, *followed by the* HEADMISTRESS. *Camera tracks in after them. (Still on page 2)*

HEADMISTRESS *opening the door* : In you go. . . .

JEAN-LOUIS *goes down on one knee and kisses his son.*

JEAN-LOUIS : I promise, Antoine, cross my heart . . . if you're a good boy this week, next Sunday we'll go on a boat trip.

ANTOINE : No, tomorrow.

JEAN-LOUIS : No, on Sunday. . . . Tomorrow you have to work ! On Sunday.

HEADMISTRESS *pushing the child in through the door* : Go and have your dinner, Antoine. . . . Off you go. . . .

ANTOINE *goes in. The* HEADMISTRESS *and* JEAN-LOUIS *come slowly down the steps towards the car. Camera pans to follow them.*

HEADMISTRESS *with a sigh* : You spoil him.

JEAN-LOUIS : Well . . . it's only once a week.

HEADMISTRESS : But he doesn't do much work you know. . . . He's lazy. He's intelligent . . . oh yes, he's intelligent all right . . . but very lazy.

JEAN-LOUIS : You know where he gets it from of course.

HEADMISTRESS : I see. . . . And what are you going to do about it?

JEAN-LOUIS : Well . . . I sent him to you two years ago, and you've looked after him marvellously for two years. . . . I am

21

sure you can do even better in the future.

HEADMISTRESS *sighing*: And throughout those two years I've never been able to have a serious conversation with you.

JEAN-LOUIS *getting into the Mustang*: I'm sorry, but I've never been able to have a serious conversation with a beautiful woman.

The HEADMISTRESS *simpers.* JEAN-LOUIS *turns on the headlamps, starts the engine and presses a button to close the hood.*

HEADMISTRESS: Drive carefully, I think there's going to be some fog this evening . . . and there may be ice on the roads.

JEAN-LOUIS *leaning out of the car*: Ice?

HEADMISTRESS: Yes.

She steps back to let the car move off, and notices with surprise someone in the shadows a little way away.

HEADMISTRESS: Are you still here then? *She goes off.*

Camera pans with the Mustang as it turns in the driveway.

HEADMISTRESS *reappearing*: Monsieur Duroc . . . wait a minute!

She goes up to the car, which has stopped. JEAN-LOUIS *gets out as* ANNE *approaches, looking slightly embarrassed.*

Theme music. In the following scene, also shot through a blue filter, we are inside the moving Mustang, at night. It is raining.

24. Medium close-up of JEAN-LOUIS' *right hand on the steering wheel. The camera is facing the windscreen and the dashboard, and we can see part of* JEAN-LOUIS' *body, out of focus on the left. The dazzle of approaching headlamps and the movement of the wipers form a constantly changing pattern on the rain-swept windscreen.*

25. Medium close-up of JEAN-LOUIS *in profile, talking as he drives. (Still on page 2) His voice is covered by the theme music.*

26. Medium close-up of ANNE, *from the side, sitting in the passenger seat, smiling across at* JEAN-LOUIS.

27. Medium shot of the two of them facing us through the windscreen. (Still on page 2)

22

JEAN-LOUIS : Do you often miss your train?

ANNE : Yes, quite often. I'm not very punctual on the whole.

28. Reverse shot from inside the car. The view is obscured by squalls of rain and the sweep of the windscreen wiper.

JEAN-LOUIS *off* : And do you always find someone to drive you back?

29. Another shot of the two of them facing us through the windscreen.

ANNE : No, no . . . I stay the night in Deauville. *A pause.* . . . No, she doesn't work very hard. *She smiles.*

JEAN-LOUIS : I know. . . .

30. A slightly longer shot of them.

JEAN-LOUIS : . . . she's intelligent but lazy.

ANNE *turning to him* : Who told you that?

JEAN-LOUIS : Aha! . . . *They look at each other and laugh.*

31. Close-up of JEAN-LOUIS *driving.*

JEAN-LOUIS : What's her name?

32. Close-up of ANNE.

ANNE : Françoise . . . *She turns to* JEAN-LOUIS, *smiling.* . . . and him?

33. Resume on JEAN-LOUIS.

JEAN-LOUIS : Antoine.

ANNE *off* : Antoine . . . that's nice.

Camera pans away from JEAN-LOUIS *to* ANNE, *who smiles to herself.*

34. Reverse shot, showing the street outside through the windscreen of the moving car. They are going through a small town whose streets are illuminated with festive strings of lights.

JEAN-LOUIS *off* : Do you come to the school regularly?

ANNE *off* : Yes . . . I come every week, when I'm not working. *A pause.* And you?

JEAN-LOUIS *off* : Oh yes. I come every Saturday, and sometimes on Sunday as well.*

35. Medium close-up of ANNE *in profile, silent and lost in thought.*

36. Another shot of her from the front, through the wind-

---

* End of the first reel, 438 metres.

screen. She sighs. Noise of a car passing in the opposite direction; its headlamps sweep across. A pause, then ANNE *points at the dashboard.*

ANNE : May I?

Zoom back to include JEAN-LOUIS. *As he replies, he presses a button on the dashboard radio, out of frame.*

JEAN-LOUIS : Oh. . . . Yes, of course.

A quavering voice comes from the radio, singing a popular song, full of pathos, of pre-World War One vintage. ANNE *starts to laugh.*

ANNE : Oh! . . . Excuse me.

37. Close-up of JEAN-LOUIS. *He glances sideways at* ANNE.

38. Medium close-up of the two of them through the windscreen, listening to the song. ANNE *suppresses a giggle and looks at* JEAN-LOUIS, *who turns at the same instant. They grin at each other.*

39. Medium close-up of her, trying not to laugh and rubbing her nose.

40. Close-up of JEAN-LOUIS *watching her.*

41. Close-up of ANNE *smiling.*

42. Medium close-up of JEAN-LOUIS *grinning broadly.*

43. Close-up of ANNE. *She glances at* JEAN-LOUIS.

44. Close-up of JEAN-LOUIS. *He looks down at the radio on the dashboard, then grins across at* ANNE *as she finally bursts out laughing, off.*

JEAN-LOUIS *laughing himself*: You mustn't laugh. . . . Songs like that made people cry back in 1914.

Camera pans slowly across to ANNE.

ANNE *with mock seriousness*: Oh . . . did they! . . .

45. Medium close-up of the two of them through the windscreen as the song continues. They exchange glances and smile.

46. Medium close-up of JEAN-LOUIS, *grinning broadly.*

47. Medium close-up of ANNE *doing likewise.*

48. Close-up of JEAN-LOUIS, *driving fairly fast, keeping his eyes on the road. The headlights of an approaching car can be seen through the rear window. Long pause.*

49. Another shot of JEAN-LOUIS *and* ANNE *through the windscreen; the wipers are now stationary.*

JEAN-LOUIS : Are you married?

ANNE *with a strange smile*: Yes. . . . *A pause.* Yes, yes!
. . . And you?

JEAN-LOUIS : Oh yes. . . .

ANNE *turning to him*: You don't look like a married man.

    *50. Medium close-up of her looking at him closely, then
smiling.*

JEAN-LOUIS *off*: What's a married man supposed to look like
then?

    51. Medium close-up of him.

JEAN-LOUIS : And what does your husband do?

    52. Resume on ANNE *smiling pensively.*

   .   .   .   .

*In the next scene, which is a flashback in normal colour,
we are in what appears to be a film set of a Far West
township.**

*53. Close-up of the lower half of a man's face, unshaven,
smoking a cigar. It is* PIERRE, ANNE'S *husband. Various
country sounds, especially bird-song.*

54. Medium close-up of PIERRE *in profile, wearing a black
stetson and a red neckerchief.*

*55. Another shot of him facing the camera, playing a
typical B-Western baddie. (Still on page 3) A horse is
partly visible to one side of him. Complete silence apart
from a few bird noises in the distance.*

56. Close-up of PIERRE'S *face from below, still smoking
the cigar.*

*57. Close-up of two young women in back view, watch-
ing* PIERRE, *who is standing near his horse in the background, his hand on his gun. The young women exchange
horrified glances.*

58. Close-up of PIERRE'S *hand on his revolver.*

59. Low angle medium close-up of another COWBOY
*sitting on a rail, his hand also on his gun. Only the lower
part of his body is visible.*

60. Reverse angle medium shot, the COWBOY *on the rail
in the foreground, three-quarters back to camera,* PIERRE

---

* In fact it is the cowboy village of Ermenonville in an amusement park
near Paris.

facing him in the background.
Voice *off* : Gunfight!
The Cowboy *leaps from the rail and fires.* Pierre *draws his gun and pulls the trigger. Nothing happens.*
61. Medium shot of Pierre. *He tries to fire the gun again, then throws it on the ground in disgust.*
62. Long shot of the street: to the right is the saloon and opposite, on the left, a shop with a sign saying ' Levis '. The shot is framed in the foreground by the rails of a wooden fence and a couple of cart wheels lying on the ground. Camera pans left as a group of women, dressed in period costume and carrying parasols, come down the slope from the saloon to where Pierre *and three other men are carrying out an animated post-mortem on the gunfight. End of flashback.*

. . . .

63. Blue filter. Resume on Jean-Louis *in close-up, seen through the windscreen of the moving Mustang.*
Jean-Louis : So he's an actor?
64. Medium close-up of the two of them.
Anne : Yes. . . . *With a far-away look.* At least not exactly . . . he's not only an actor.

. . . .

65. Another flashback, normal colour. Medium close-up of a car windscreen from inside, Pierre *in back view at the wheel. The screen shatters and the sunlit country outside whirls round as the car rolls over and over with an earsplitting noise.*
66. The noise continues. Low angle medium shot of the car — a white Fiat — rolling over and over, the doors flying open.
67. Low angle medium shot of another car crashing into two others, going away from camera and bursting into flames.
68. Another shot of the same crash from the side.
69. A closer shot of the car bursting into flames.
70. Another similar shot. Red and orange flames fill the screen.

. . . .

26

71. Blue filter. Resume on close-up of JEAN-LOUIS *in the Mustang. It is raining hard and the wipers sweep to and fro.*

JEAN-LOUIS : A stunt man . . . that's an odd profession. Tell me, how does one get to know a stunt man? *Pan to medium close-up of* ANNE. JEAN-LOUIS *continues off.* At the bottom of a ravine? *She looks at him sadly and shakes her head. Camera pans back to* JEAN-LOUIS. In a burning aeroplane?

72. Medium close-up of the two of them through the windscreen. The bonnet is awash with rain.

JEAN-LOUIS : Am I getting warm?

ANNE *turning to him :* No.

JEAN-LOUIS : Tell me.

.   .   .   .

73. Flashback, normal colour. Low angle close-up of PIERRE, *kissing a black girl who is leaning against the dark, almost grey-green wall of a castle.*

74. Music. Low angle medium close-up of ANNE *wearing a sheepskin jacket, sitting near a tree which stands out against blue sky. She watches the scene, glancing at a stop-watch and smiling happily.*

75. Resume on PIERRE *in medium close-up. Pan left as he moves away from the girl, carrying a coffin, then stops and looks back.*

76. A slightly longer shot of the same scene. Pan to follow him as, hamming madly, he prances away from the castle, spinning round with the coffin and finally reaching the edge of the film set, where there is a camera team and floodlights. A cloud of smoke hangs over the scene. The cameraman turns his camera to follow PIERRE. *Zoom forward onto* ANNE *seated on the camera truck, laughing as she watches* PIERRE, *off-screen.*

77. Low angle medium close-up of PIERRE *putting down the coffin near a man carrying a microphone boom. Pan left and tilt down as he comes over to* ANNE *and discusses the take, kneeling on the ground beside her.*

78. Low angle medium close-up of the two of them in profile, talking, ANNE *with a film script on her knee. Their dialogue is covered by the music over.*

27

*79. Medium shot of the two of them in front of the big
35mm camera, PIERRE now standing. (Still on page 3)
They are silhouetted against the floodlights and the smoke
swirls behind them.**

. . . .

*80. Blue filter. Resume on close-up of JEAN-LOUIS in the
Mustang at night, seen through the windscreen. Noise of
passing cars and effect of their lights; the windscreen
wipers sweep to and fro.*
JEAN-LOUIS : He sounds like something out of a novel. Apart
from the stunt man bit, it's not very original.
ANNE *off at first* : Oh, I don't claim to be original. *Camera
pans slowly across to her.* After all, people meet, get married,
have a child . . . they're things which can happen to anyone.
It's the person one loves who can be original.
JEAN-LOUIS *off* : And your husband is original?
ANNE : Yes, for me. He's so exciting, so exclusive . . . *She
smiles happily.* . . . so complete. He goes wild over things,
people . . . ideas.
JEAN-LOUIS : You make him sound like Christ.
ANNE *looking at him* : Perhaps he is for me . . . for instance,
I lived for a week in Brazil without ever having been there.
Pan to JEAN-LOUIS. *She continues off.* Pierre made a film down
there. When he came back he talked about nothing but the
samba for a week. The samba became a part of our life.
JEAN-LOUIS *with an odd smile* : The samba became part of
your life!

. . . .

Flashback to PIERRE *and* ANNE'S *apartment, normal
colour. Throughout the 'Samba Saravah', sung and
sometimes recited by* PIERRE, *a succession of scenes show
the couple's life together.*
81. As PIERRE *begins to sing, accompanied by an
orchestra, off, close-up of him facing the camera. Zoom
backwards to show him seated in an armchair reading a
comic called 'The Ghost Town'. He is wearing a white*

---

* Judging by the stills taken on the set, Lelouch seems to have shot
several different versions of the castle scene.

bathrobe. Camera continues to move backwards, reveal-
ing ANNE *at a table in the foreground, serving up break-*
fast.

SONG ' *Samba Saravah* ' :
    ' Happiness is more or less what we seek.
    I like to laugh and sing and I don't speak
    Against nice people having a good time . . .'
    82. Close-up of ANNE'S *hands massaging* PIERRE'S *head*
as she gives him a shampoo, then zoom back to show the
two of them, PIERRE *kneeling in front of the washbasin,*
ANNE *standing.*

SONG *continued* :
    ' Yet if a samba leaves no sadness over
    It's like a wine which leaves you stone-cold sober.
    It's like a wine which leaves you stone-cold sober.
    No that is not the samba I'll call mine.'
    83. Close-up of a french window at the side of a farm-
house in the Camargue. PIERRE *comes out, wearing a*
suède jacket, and camera tracks back as he comes towards
ANNE, *who is stretched out on the grass, doing exercises in*
the sunshine. He circles round her.

SONG *continued, the words spoken* : ' " Doing a samba without sadness is like loving a woman who is no more than
beautiful " . . . these are the very words of Vinicius de
Moraes, poet and diplomat, author of this song, and, as he
says himself, the blackest white man in Brazil.'
    84. Medium shot of PIERRE *on a prancing white horse*
in the Camargue, a stretch of water behind him.
    85. Low angle medium shot of a pair of red gates at the
entrance to a bull ring, a young bull bounding around in
the foreground. Camera zooms out to long shot as PIERRE
rides in through the gate, then pans with him as he gallops
around the ring, making passes at the bull. He rides off.

SONG *continued, spoken words* : ' I, who am perhaps the most
Brazilian Frenchman in France — I would like to tell you
about my love for the samba like a lover who, not daring to
talk to the one he loves, talks about her to everyone he meets.'
    86. Low angle medium shot of PIERRE *riding up to*
ANNE, *who is also on horseback, behind the barrier at*

the side of the ring.
[Long shot, slight high angle, of PIERRE *and* ANNE
galloping across the Camargue.*]
87. *Medium close-up of the two of them, in profile,
facing each other across a table laden with the remains
of a meal. There are plates of cheese, fruit, a bottle
of Châteauneuf-du-Pape. Camera tracks out slowly as*
PIERRE, *continuing to sing, feeds* ANNE *a piece of orange,
then another. (Still on page 4) They gaze lovingly at
each other. After a while* PIERRE *pours out some more
wine without taking his eyes off* ANNE. *She drinks.*
SONG *continued, the words sung* :
    ' I know some people who find songs a bore.
    For others they're a fashion and nothing more,
    And for still others money's the only thing . . .'
88. *Close-up of* PIERRE'S *fingers on the strings of a
guitar.* ANNE'S *arm reaches across. Zoom back to show
him seated on a sofa, in the living room, wearing a base-
ball cap.* ANNE *turns to a sink behind* PIERRE, *apparently
washing up.***
SONG *continued, the words sung* :
    ' I love them and the world I've been around,
    Searching out their roots on foreign ground.
    Today if the deepest roots are to be found,
    Then it's the samba-song that we must sing.'
89. *Exterior long shot of the two of them, riding side by
side across the Camargue. Camera tracks and pans with
them as they splash through a swamp, beds of rushes in
the foreground. The song continues over a series of
tracking shots of riders on horseback.*
SONG *continued, words spoken* : ' João Gilberto, Carlos Libra,
Doryval Carpmi, Antonio Carlos Jobim, Vinicius de Moraes,
Baden Powel, who composed the music for this song, and all
the others, greetings.'
90. *A closer shot of the two of them splashing through*

---

* This shot was mentioned in l'Avant-Scène's version of the script, but it
was not seen in the English print of the film.
** They are in fact in the open-plan living room typical of a contem-
porary Camargue dwelling.

the swamp, camera tracking with them. (Still on page 4)
91. Tracking shot of horses' legs splashing through the
water.
92. Medium tracking shot of five people on horseback,
amongst whom are PIERRE *and* ANNE, *holding hands.*
[*Another long shot: the riders pass behind a herd of bulls*
led by a herdsman.*]
93. Low angle medium shot: PIERRE, *leaving* ANNE *behind*
for a moment, rides forward to offer the others small
cigars.

SONG *continued, words spoken* : ' Tonight I would like to get
drunk so that I can rave all the more about the people I have
found, thanks to you, and who have made the samba what it
is. Saravah, Peigin, Noel Rosa, Dolores Duran, Silvio Mon-
teiro, and many others, and all those to come . . .'

94. Resume on the couple side by side: ANNE *leans*
towards PIERRE, *holding his hand. Camera pans left as*
it tracks, losing them.
95. Resume on the two of them. ANNE *removes some-*
thing from PIERRE'S *eye as they continue to ride, camera*
tracking with them.
96. Medium long shot of the two of them, a herd of bulls
passing in the foreground.
97. Medium close-up of the group of riders from the
side, camera tracking with them as they now gallop along
at top speed. The song continues over the next two long,
fast tracking shots.
98. Long shot, tracking very fast with the herd of bulls,
who are now stampeding; beds of rushes are seen as a
blur of colour in the foreground.
99. Similar shot of the riders galloping in pursuit, partly
obscured by the rushes.

SONG *continued, words spoken* : ' Edu Lobo and my friends
who are with me tonight — Baden, of course, Ico, Oswaldo,
Luigi, Oscar, Nicolino, Milton. . . . *A pause.* Saravah . . .
Saravah ! All those thanks to whom there is a word I shall
never be able to say again without a thrill . . . a word which

---

* Mentioned in l'Avant-Scène's script, but not seen in the English print
of the film.

moves a whole people and makes them sing with their hands raised to the sky . . . Samba.'

100. Medium shot of ANNE *from above, wearing a black evening dress, climbing a wooden staircase. Camera tilts up, panning with her as she comes face to face with* PIERRE, *in a dinner jacket, leaning against some bookshelves on the landing. She passes in front of him, and he follows her to the door of the bedroom, camera panning with them. They go in.*

SONG *continued, words sung* :
  ' It first came from Bahia, rumour goes.
  Its rhythm and its poetry it owes
  To centuries of dancing and of pain . . .'

101. Close-up of the two of them in the bedroom, kissing. ANNE *takes off* PIERRE'S *jacket. Slow zoom back as* ANNE *throws the jacket on the bed and turns to let* PIERRE *undo her dress.*

SONG *continued, words sung* :
  ' But whatever the feelings it combines,
  Although it may be white in form and rhymes,
  Though it be white in form and rhymes,
  Its heart is black as black and that is plain.'

102. Medium shot of the two of them. ANNE *is lying on the bed, facing camera, reading a book of comic strips — the adventures of ' Bicot'. (Still on page 4)* PIERRE *is nearest camera, in profile, wearing a bathrobe, playing a guitar.*

SONG *continued, words sung* :
  ' But whatever the feelings it combines,
  Although it may be white in form and rhymes,
  Though it be white in form and rhymes,
  Its heart is black as black and that is plain.'

Zoom back to show PIERRE *seated in front of a typewriter. From time to time he types out the words of the song he is composing.*

SONG *continued, words sung* :
  ' But whatever the feelings it combines,
  Although it may be white in form and rhymes,
  Though it be white in form and rhymes,

32

Its heart is black as black and that is plain.'
As he comes to the end of the song, Pierre *gets up, puts down his guitar and goes over to* Anne *on the bed. He leans over and kisses her. Slow zoom in.*

. . . . . .

103. Blue filter. Close-up of Jean-Louis *in profile, at the wheel of the Mustang. He grins across at* Anne. *The song fades out on the refrain and we hear only the noise of the rain outside.*

Song, *sung by* Pierre, *off* :
' Its heart is black as black and that is plain. . . .'
104. Close-up of Anne *in profile, looking across at him. She turns with a sad smile.*
105. Close-up of Jean-Louis, *from behind, driving.*
Jean-Louis : Where shall I drop you . . . when we get to Paris?
106. Close-up of Anne *suppressing her grief.*
Anne : The rue Lamarck.
Jean-Louis *off* : Rue Lamarck? Where's that?
Anne *smiling* : In the 18th.
107. Long shot of a Paris street at night. Camera pans left as traffic roars along a boulevard.*
108. The blue filter continues. Shot of the Mustang stopping in front of an apartment house: No. 14, rue Lamarck.
109. Medium close-up of the two of them seen through the windscreen.
Jean-Louis : Is this it?
Anne : Yes.
Jean-Louis *at a loss for something to say* : That's funny, I didn't know the rue Lamarck.
110. Medium close-up of the two of them seen through the side window of the car, Jean-Louis *nearest camera,* Anne *turned towards him.*
Anne : Oh, didn't you? . . . Well, it was in this street that,

---

* End of the second reel, about 350 metres. We should point out that the commercial prints of the film were composed of large reels, about 600 metres in length, each containing two of the original reels. This is therefore the end of the first commercial reel.

33

a little before 1917, Jean-Gabriel Domergue took on a Russian servant. JEAN-LOUIS *is silent.* He was called Vladimir Ulianov.
JEAN-LOUIS : Oh?
ANNE : And a year later he found out it was Lenin. *She smiles at him and turns to open the door.* Well, thank you very much for bringing me back. *She gets out.* No, no . . . please don't bother.

> *Zoom slowly back as she gets out of the car. She slams the door and stands in front of the Mustang.*

ANNE : Goodbye.
JEAN-LOUIS *opening his door and leaning out* : Hey . . . I say. *She comes round the car towards him.* I'll be going back to Deauville next Sunday . . . if you would like a lift . . . and anyway . . . *Camera zooms in to extreme close-up of his face* . . . I'd be happy to meet your husband.

.   .   .   .

> *111. Flashback, normal colour. Exterior shot of a film location in sunlit countryside. We see a tree, as a bomb explodes beside it with flames and smoke.*
> *112–117. Series of six very fast shots of explosions. Flames and smoke and appropriate noises.*
> *118. Wide shot of the battlefield, with explosions continuing right, left and centre. A soldier dressed in GI uniform, and carrying a submachine gun, moves away from camera, disappearing into the smoke. Slow zoom in as he does so.*

DIRECTOR *off* : Cut. Right, we'll retake that straight away.

> *The DIRECTOR, with his back to the camera, walks towards the soldier as he emerges from the smoke. It is PIERRE.*

PIERRE : Okay.

> *Slow zoom back as ANNE also comes into frame, and stands facing PIERRE beside the DIRECTOR. Behind them the smoke from the explosions clears slightly, revealing blue sky.*

DIRECTOR : That wasn't bad . . . but the next time don't take so many risks. Okay?

> *Zoom back further to include a 35mm movie camera and camera crew.*
> *119. Reverse angle medium close-up of PIERRE in GI*

34

*uniform standing on a bank with his back to us, looking
at the camera and camera crew in the background. Standing just below him are* ANNE *and the* DIRECTOR. *The
latter gestures to* ANNE *and starts to move away.* ANNE
stays by PIERRE, *who takes off his helmet and jumps down
from the bank.*
*120. Reverse shot: we see the three of them in low angle
medium shot from the front, with a burnt-out tree behind
them. The* DIRECTOR *moves out of frame while* PIERRE
kisses ANNE *affectionately. Then camera pans right round
to reverse shot as she runs back to the movie camera, and
the* DIRECTOR *waves his arm in the air and shouts.*

DIRECTOR *shouting* : Go !
SOUND ENGINEER *bellowing* : Silence !
Noise of explosions, machine-guns etc.
121. Reverse angle long shot of PIERRE, *having replaced
his helmet, as he dashes across the battlefield, avoiding
the falling bombs. Slow zoom in. Suddenly he gives a
long-drawn-out cry.*
122. Reverse angle medium close-up of the DIRECTOR
and ANNE *as they rush towards him in alarm, camera
panning left with them. (Still on page 4)*

.   .   .   .

*123. Resume on the rue Lamarck at night, blue filter.
Close-up of* ANNE *with sadness in her eyes. A pause.*
124. Medium close-up of JEAN-LOUIS *and* ANNE *standing
face to face at the door of the apartment house,* ANNE
three-quarters facing camera. (Still on page 4)

JEAN-LOUIS : I'm very sorry. You talked about him so light-
heartedly that I never imagined he was dead.
ANNE *turning away and pressing the doorbell* : Thank you for
offering to take me on Sunday . . . *She goes in and stops in
the doorway* . . . but I don't know if I shall be free. Anyway,
if you would like to telephone me on Saturday at midday, I'll
be able to tell you.
*Zoom back to medium shot of the two of them in the
doorway, taking in the Mustang in the foreground.*
JEAN-LOUIS : I don't know your telephone number.
ANNE : Montmartre 15-40.

JEAN-LOUIS : Goodnight.
ANNE *shutting the door* : Goodnight.
Pan to follow JEAN-LOUIS *as he goes and gets into his car. The Mustang moves off then stops, camera panning with it.*
125. Camera pans to follow JEAN-LOUIS' *hand in close-up as he opens the glove-box and takes out a piece of paper. Pan back again as he draws the paper towards him and notes down the telephone number.*
JEAN-LOUIS *to himself* : Montmartre 15-40.

126. Loud music. Normal colour. Low angle shot of the Mustang moving along a road past camera, its headlamps shining yellow in the darkness.
127. Another similar shot. The headlamps light up a hoarding as the car rounds a bend. The scene is bathed in blueish light as dawn approaches.
[*Shot of the road through the windscreen.**]
128. Low angle long shot of the entrance to the test track at Montlhéry: the Mustang comes slowly towards the camera and stops at a barrier across the road. The barrier is raised and camera pans left to follow the car as it comes and stops in front of the Ford building.
129. Medium shot of a lorry: some mechanics open the back and roll a Formula 1 single-seater down a ramp onto the track. Pan right to JEAN-LOUIS *as he gets out of the Mustang in medium close-up and looks across at the car which he is to test-drive. Another* DRIVER *comes up to him and they converse.*
130. Very high angle long shot of the track in the blue dawn light. The mechanics wheel the Formula 1 alongside a Ford GT sports-racing car, on which more mechanics are at work.
131. Medium shot of JEAN-LOUIS *and the* CHIEF MECHANIC *leaning over the open engine-hatch of the GT, in earnest discussion. The first rays of sun break through the clouds in the background.*

---

* This shot was mentioned in l'Avant-Scène's version of the script, but was not seen in the English print of the film.

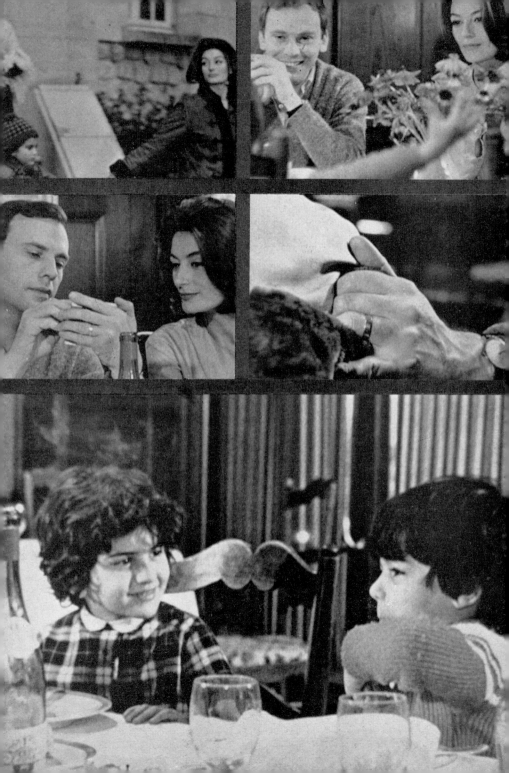

132. Long shot of the cars on the track, the administra-
tion buildings and grandstand behind.
133. High angle medium close-up of JEAN-LOUIS *and*
the CHIEF MECHANIC *bent over the engine of the GT.*
134. Another similar shot of them looking in through
one of the doors, which is open.
135. Medium shot of a MECHANIC *at work on the*
Formula 1, the GT in the background.
136. Medium close-up of JEAN-LOUIS *and the* CHIEF
MECHANIC, *seen over the roof of the GT, talking ani-*
matedly. We do not hear their voices, which are covered
by the loud music.
137. Medium close-up of them leaning over the engine
again. They straighten and the CHIEF MECHANIC *makes*
a gesture indicating ' all systems go '.
138. Medium close-up of the two of them from the side,
reflected in the windows of one of the buildings.
139. Medium close-up of JEAN-LOUIS *and the other*
DRIVER, *leaning towards each other across the roof of*
the GT, conversing. The music continues.
140. Low angle medium shot of the GT from the front,
the two drivers and the CHIEF ENGINEER *leaning over*
the engine at the back.
141. Medium close-up of a MECHANIC *raising a jack*
under the rear of the single-seater. Camera pans right to
show two more about to remove the engine cover.
142. Low angle medium close-up of the mechanics
removing the engine cover.
143. Another similar shot as they remove the front part
of the bodywork. Camera pans with them as they walk
away from the car and start to lay it on the ground.
144. High angle medium close-up of the mechanics now
working on the engine of the Formula 1.
145. Medium shot of JEAN-LOUIS *and the other* DRIVER
coming out of one of the buildings, dressed in Ford
drivers' overalls and carrying crash-helmets. (Still on
page 37) We see them coming towards us, shot through
a telephoto lens. Camera pans and tracks out in front of
them as, deep in conversation, the two men walk towards

41

the GT. A ray of sunlight breaks through.
*146. Medium shot, panning with the two men as they
come up to the GT. JEAN-LOUIS engages the CHIEF
MECHANIC in conversation, while the other DRIVER goes
off.*
*147. Medium close-up of the CHIEF MECHANIC and
JEAN-LOUIS yelling in each other's ears over the noise of
the engine, which is still covered by the soundtrack music.
JEAN-LOUIS puts on his crash-helmet.*
*148. Medium close-up of JEAN-LOUIS from the side,
fastening his helmet, a MECHANIC bending over the
engine behind him.*
*149. Medium close-up from inside the car. JEAN-LOUIS
gets in, still listening to the CHIEF MECHANIC, who bends
down and talks to him through the open door. (Still on
page 37) The CHIEF MECHANIC slams the door. The
music cuts out and we hear the noise of the engine.*
*150. High angle medium shot of the car moving slowly
onto the track. (Still on page 37) The engine misfires at
low revs. Camera tracks out as the car begins to move
faster, then the exhaust note hardens and it leaps away
under full acceleration.*
*151. Long shot, panning round with the car as it enters
a curve at the top of the banked track. We hear the gear
changes as it gathers speed.*
*152. Medium close-up of JEAN-LOUIS' gloved hands on
the steering wheel.*
*153. Close-up of the rear-view mirror, with the curved
track streaking by outside.*
*154. Medium close-up of JEAN-LOUIS in profile, driving
with great concentration, carefully judging his gear-
changes.*
155. Close-up of his head and shoulders.
*156. Resume on medium close-up of his hands on the
steering wheel. He takes them off to test the car's stability.
(Still on page 37) It is raining slightly and the wipers
are going very fast.*
*157. High angle long shot of the car streaking round a
curve towards camera.*

42

158. Close-up of JEAN-LOUIS *removing his hands from the wheel again. The wheel vibrates, the car bucks continually.*

159. Long shot, zooming in on the car as it enters another curve.

160. Resume on JEAN-LOUIS, *his hands off the wheel.*

161. Fast pan left and zoom out as the GT streaks round a curve towards camera.

162. Resume on JEAN-LOUIS.

163. Long shot of the car rounding another curve, away from camera.

164. Long shot and zoom in as it comes towards camera again.

165. Medium long shot, panning left with the car as it travels round the banking. Trees flash past in the foreground.

166. Similar shot of a white Mustang bearing the number 184, lit by the rising sun.

167. Resume on the GT. The engine misfires as JEAN-LOUIS *slows down to keep pace with the Mustang.*

168. Resume on the Mustang. Camera tilts up to include the GT travelling just above it on the banking. (Still on page 37) The GT draws away again, camera still panning.

169. Similar shot of the GT by itself, accelerating.

170. Another panning shot. The GT passes the Mustang again.

171. Resume on the Mustang by itself, accelerating.

172. A longer shot, panning with the two cars. The trees in the centre of the track can now be clearly seen.

173. Close-up of a jerrycan being emptied into the fuel tank of the stationary GT. Camera pans across the windscreen, through which JEAN-LOUIS *can be seen talking to his fellow* DRIVER *in the passenger seat, to show another jerrycan being emptied into the tank on the other side. There is a sudden silence after the noise of the car engines, and the voice of a* RADIO COMMENTATOR *is heard off. His voice continues over the next series of shots, accompanied by sounds of banging etc. from the mechanics at work on the cars.*

43

Radio Commentator *off* : . . . he said that he would, moreover, give a press conference on the subject of the increases. And now we will pass on to sport, a subject which as you know is almost entirely dominated by the Monte-Carlo Rally, the 35th of that name, which is due to start in eight days' time. And of course everywhere the teams are preparing their cars for the coming contest, which in view of the weather promises to be a particularly tough one. . . .

174. As the Commentator *talks we see a* Mechanic *in low angle medium close-up from below, rolling a wheel along, camera panning with him. The sun is now setting.*
175. Close-up of him fixing it on one of the cars.
176. Close-up of one of the headlamps of the white Mustang, at dusk. A hand points at it.
177. Low angle medium close-up of two mechanics silhouetted against the twilit sky, adjusting the other headlamp.
178. Low angle long shot of the white Mustang streaking past the grandstand at night, headlamps ablaze.
179. High angle long shot. Camera pans right as the Mustang sweeps past, accompanied by the GT.
180. Medium shot, tracking out in front of the Mustang. The voice of the Commentator *continues.*

Radio Commentator *off* : Among the favourites are the Toivonen and Makinen crews, running in a Cooper and DS21 respectively. . . . We know that they have been practising very hard in the past week and are finishing off the last . . .

His voice is drowned by the roar of engines as a series of rapid shots gives the atmosphere of another night's work at the track.
181. Medium close-up of Jean-Louis' *co-driver,* Henri Chemin, *standing by the open bonnet of the white Mustang, which they will drive in the Monte Carlo Rally. Camera pans across the bonnet to show* Jean-Louis *on the other side. Noise of an engine being revved in bursts.*
182. Medium close-up of Jean-Louis, *in profile, watching the* Chief Mechanic *removing the air-filter from the Mustang's engine.*

44

183. Close-up of JEAN-LOUIS *in profile, talking, his voice covered by the noise of the engine.*
184. High angle close-up of the arms of JEAN-LOUIS *and the* CHIEF MECHANIC *reaching down into the engine. (Still on page 37)*
185. Close-up of their heads in profile, bent over the engine, CHEMIN *looking on in the background.*
186. High angle medium close-up of the CHIEF MECHANIC'S *arm as he adjusts the engine.*
187. Medium close-up of JEAN-LOUIS *addressing the* CHIEF MECHANIC, *who is bent over the engine in the foreground.*
188. Long shot of JEAN-LOUIS *on the track, surrounded by mechanics and engineers.*
189. Medium close-up of JEAN-LOUIS *wearing glasses, with his crash-helmet on, watching another car circulating.**
190. Long shot, panning with the Mustang as it streaks along the track, headlamps ablaze, accompanied by the GT.
191. Another day dawns. Medium shot of the Ford building: in front of it the mechanics and engineers stand beside JEAN-LOUIS *as he watches the cars circulate, stopwatch in hand. Another Ford GT stands behind them.*
A MECHANIC : What d'you mean, not good?
JEAN-LOUIS : One-seventeen. *Camera re-frames slightly. A car flashes past in front of them, a blur of white.* Forty-three-four.
A MECHANIC : Not bad, huh?
JEAN-LOUIS *speaking into a walkie-talkie* : Yes. . . . What revs are you at now? *A pause.* 11,000? *Camera re-frames. The car goes past again.* Forty-three-seven. What revs now? *A pause.* 10,300.
A MECHANIC : So we've gained; 200 revs, that's good!
192. Medium shot of JEAN-LOUIS *getting into the Formula 1 single-seater. Its engine revs in bursts.* CHEMIN *helps him on with the visor of his crash-helmet. (Still on page 37)*

---

* End of the third reel, about 325 metres.

193. High angle close-up of the steering wheel and dash-board. JEAN-LOUIS' *gloved hand points at the rev-counter.*
194. Close-up of JEAN-LOUIS *with the* CHIEF MECHANIC *bending over him, shouting some last-minute advice in his ear, his voice drowned by the noise of the engine.*
195. Low angle medium shot. Camera pans left as the single-seater moves off.
196. Medium close-up of JEAN-LOUIS *at the wheel, the camera on the front of the car. It shoots under a Dunlop bridge over the track.*
197. Close-up of JEAN-LOUIS *driving, looking tense.*
198. Medium shot of two mechanics standing by the track as the car sweeps past.
199. Similar shot of CHEMIN *in back view, wearing a crash-helmet. He waves his arm, signalling to* JEAN-LOUIS *to let the car right out. It passes, accelerating.*
200. Low angle medium shot of CHEMIN *and two of the engineers standing by the pits in front of the Ford GT. The single-seater flashes past in the foreground.*
201. A longer shot of the same scene. Everyone urges the single-seater on as it flashes past once more.
202. High angle medium long shot of JEAN-LOUIS *as he gets out of the Formula 1 near the building and is greeted by* CHEMIN. JEAN-LOUIS *walks away, taking off his crash-helmet. Camera pans right, revealing that the scene is shot through the window of the timing post.* JEAN-LOUIS *enters by the door and camera pans back as he sits down by the window.* CHEMIN *gets into the Formula 1, seen in soft focus through the window.* JEAN-LOUIS *takes a piece of paper out of his pocket, pauses for a moment, then lifts the telephone receiver. (Still on page 37)*
JEAN-LOUIS : Mademoiselle, can you get me Montmartre 15-40 please? . . . *He looks at his watch.* Hallo? No, no, can you get it in five minutes, please? *He hangs up.*
203. A longer shot of the same scene. JEAN-LOUIS *lights a cigarette, undoes his jacket and turns to watch the track through the window. Zoom forwards as the Formula 1 prepares to move off. The phone rings. Zoom back to show* JEAN-LOUIS *again as he lifts the receiver.*

46

JEAN-LOUIS *a little nervously*: Hello, Montmartre 15-40?
. . . Jean-Louis Duroc speaking. I gave you a lift from Paris
to D . . . um . . . from Deauville to Paris last Sunday. Yes,
how are you? *A pause.* Well, you see, er . . . tomorrow I'm
going back to visit my son at the school, so I thought, if you
like, I could give you a lift. *A pause.* Oh, whatever time you
like . . . er . . . oh, I don't know . . . nine o'clock, nine-
thirty . . . as you wish. *Pan towards the window as the car
sets off outside.* JEAN-LOUIS *continues off.* Nine o'clock? . . .
All right, nine o'clock.

*204. Medium shot panning with the red Mustang as it
drives up the rue Lamarck in the daytime and double
parks in front of number 14.* JEAN-LOUIS *gets out, glances
across at the apartment house and starts to walk to and
fro, looking at his watch. Birds twitter, a dog barks. After
a moment he takes off his jacket, puts it in the back of the
car and seats himself at the wheel again.*
*205. Medium close-up of him through the windscreen
on which, despite the dull weather, are reflected a few
early rays of sun. As he waits he reads ' Le Nouvel
Observateur '.*
206. Medium shot, the car in the foreground. Behind it,
ANNE *comes out of the apartment house and bends down
to address* JEAN-LOUIS *through the car window.*
ANNE : Good morning.
JEAN-LOUIS *immediately folds his paper and gets out.*
ANNE *looking apologetic* : I'm late.
Camera pans as JEAN-LOUIS *accompanies her round the
car and opens the door.*
JEAN-LOUIS : Oh . . . no . . . not at all . . . it could have
been worse.
She gets in and JEAN-LOUIS *closes the door.*
*207. Long shot panning with the Mustang as it moves
towards the tunnel of the motorway leading west out of
Paris. It is beginning to rain. Coming in the opposite direc-
tion there is a long queue of cars, more or less stationary.
Impatient hootings from the queue. The exit lane is free
of traffic as the Mustang disappears into the tunnel.*

47

*208. Backward tracking shot: on the motorway, wreathed
in mist under a sharp shower of rain, the Mustang moves
towards us with dipped headlamps, passes another car
and continues on its way.*
*209–217. There follows a series of nine similar backward
tracking shots of the Mustang speeding along through the
rain, the sun just breaking through the overcast sky. In
the last three shots, its headlamps are extinguished. The
voice of the* RADIO COMMENTATOR *is heard off.*

RADIO COMMENTATOR *off*: And that soothing piece of music
was as you may have guessed entitled ' Amour ', played by the
Daniel Walt orchestra. Well now, it's Sunday morning and
time, I think, to talk about the weather, which doesn't promise
to be too good today, in fact I'm afraid that according to the
weather forecast for today there will be a lot of rain. They say
there will be rain in most places . . .

218. Medium close-up of JEAN-LOUIS, *seen through the
windscreen, the wipers sweeping to and fro in front of
him. The reflections of roadside trees move across the
glass.*

RADIO COMMENTATOR *off*:. . . and flooding on the roads in
the South and Central France. As for those Parisians who are
perhaps just now getting together a little picnic for a trip to
the country . . .

219. Similar medium close-up of ANNE.

RADIO COMMENTATOR *off*: . . . well, they would do better
to stay in Paris . . . go to the cinema, have a game of cards
. . . or of course listen to the radio along with us . . . for as
you know I shall be on the air throughout the day, keeping
things going with a variety of items which I hope you will find
more or less interesting.

ANNE *looks out of the window.*

220. Medium close-up of JEAN-LOUIS *(as 218). He grins
across at* ANNE.

RADIO COMMENTATOR *off*: So here we are, it's Sunday morning, there's bad weather on all the roads . . . and we have in
fact just received a piece of news which illustrates this. . . .

*221. Medium close-up of the windscreen, the wipers
sweeping to and fro.*

48

Radio Commentator *off* : A man and a woman have just died after skidding in a powerful car.

222. Medium close-up of the two of them facing the camera, through the windscreen. The rain seems to have stopped and the wipers are at rest.

Jean-Louis : I don't like hearing things like that.

Anne : No, especially when one's in a car.

Jean-Louis : Do I drive badly?

Anne : No . . . no, you're average.

Radio Commentator *off* : And now we shall forget this sad piece of news in listening to some more light music. Here is a little piece which I am sure you won't need any help in recognising.

Anne : You still haven't told me what you do.

Jean-Louis : Well, you see, I have a job which is really very extraordinary . . . yes, very . . . original. . . . *He laughs.* . . . And it brings in a lot of money.

.   .   .   .

Loud, brassy music. We are in the streets of Montmartre in the daytime. The scene is shot in black and white through a greenish filter. As the scene progresses, Jean-Louis *is revealed dressed in a very loud white suit with a black pin stripe and a broad-brimmed trilby, a cigar clenched between his teeth.*

223. The first shot is a close-up of his hand taking bank-notes from another, feminine, hand. (Still on page 38) He hefts the pile of notes suspiciously. Pan to show the torso of a prostitute leaning provocatively against a wall. She takes another note from her bosom and hands it over. The music continues. The Girl *turns round.* Jean-Louis' *hand pats the* Girl's *bottom; camera tilts up as he touches the hand to his cheek.*

224. Medium shot of the two of them — Jean-Louis *looking every inch the pimp, a carnation in his button-hole, hard eyes and a raffish expression. Smiling sweetly, the* Girl *hands back the umbrella she has been holding while he takes the money. Apparently pleased with the takings, he walks on towards camera, which tracks out in front of him. He turns a corner and goes up to another*

49

PROSTITUTE *who takes the cigar from his mouth, and kisses him, slipping some notes into his breast pocket as she does so. (Still on page 38)*

225. Medium close-up of her hand stuffing the notes into his breast pocket.

226. Medium close-up of JEAN-LOUIS *in profile, face to face with another* GIRL. *He hands her the umbrella and, with a very blasé air, slaps her violently across the face. He motions her to turn round, and camera tilts down as he takes some more banknotes which are tucked into the waistband of her skirt. (Still on page 38) She turns to face him again, camera tilting up, and he extracts some more notes which she has hidden in her brassière. After this manoeuvre he presents his cheek, which she kisses, looking sullen. (Still on page 38)*

227. Medium shot of the two of them. The GIRL *steps back and* JEAN-LOUIS *continues towards camera, grinning broadly, immensely pleased with himself.*

. . . .

228. Normal colour. Medium close-up of ANNE *through the windscreen of the Mustang. She laughs.*

ANNE : Congratulations, that's a nice profession. But apart from that?

Camera pans to JEAN-LOUIS.

JEAN-LOUIS : I have . . . I have a cover. . . . I work in the automobile industry. . . . I test cars.

ANNE *off* : You're a racing driver?

JEAN-LOUIS : Yes.

229. Wide shot of the road, which is flooded. Two men with shotguns are riding through the water on mopeds. The Mustang comes past in the other direction, liberally splashing them in the process. (Still on page 38)

ANNE *off* : Oh, I think you've splashed someone. . . . Look. *The car moves out of frame. In the background the two men have stopped, soaked to the skin. They look furiously after the car.*

JEAN-LOUIS *off* : They're going shooting. No mercy for people like that!

230. Low angle medium shot of the entrance to the

school at Deauville. ANNE *and the* HEADMISTRESS *are standing by the doorway with* FRANÇOISE. JEAN-LOUIS' *head is seen for a moment at the bottom of frame.*

HEADMISTRESS : She had a bit of a cough at the end of the week, you know. *She arranges* FRANÇOISE'S *scarf.* I don't think it's serious but anyway she mustn't catch cold. . . . There you are.

ANNE *taking her daughter by the hand* : Come along, darling . . . are you feeling all right? *To the* HEADMISTRESS : Well, goodbye.

They start to go down the steps. (Still on page 39)

HEADMISTRESS : Ah, I thought so.

ANNE : What?

HEADMISTRESS : I said : I thought so . . . well . . . when I didn't see you . . . er . . . you didn't come off the nine o'clock train.

ANNE : Oh, yes . . . well, thank you . . . goodbye.

Pan, cutting out the HEADMISTRESS, *to follow them down the steps to where the Mustang is parked.* JEAN-LOUIS *holds the door open for them.*

HEADMISTRESS *off* : Goodbye.

JEAN-LOUIS : Goodbye, Madame.

231. Medium shot of the interior of a restaurant. The entire scene is shot in black and white through a sepia filter. We see JEAN-LOUIS *and* ANNE *sitting side by side at a table, with the two children,* ANTOINE *and* FRANÇOISE, *facing them, in back view.* JEAN-LOUIS *is smoking. On the table are salad and various hors d'oeuvres, and a small vase of flowers.*

ANNE *to the children* : Well, are you happy?

FRANÇOISE *and* ANTOINE *in chorus* : Oh, yes . . . yes . . . yes. . . .

ANNE *to* JEAN-LOUIS : Tell me about your job.

FRANÇOISE : My job?

ANNE *laughing* : No . . . not yours.

JEAN-LOUIS : Antoine, tell her about my job.

ANTOINE : What?

JEAN-LOUIS : Don't you want to tell them about my job?

51

ANTOINE : No, but I'll . . . I'll tell you all about my job.

JEAN-LOUIS : All right, tell me about your job.

ANTOINE : The one I'll have when I'm grown up?

JEAN-LOUIS : Yes, come on, tell us. *He grins at* ANNE.

ANTOINE : I want to be a fireman!

JEAN-LOUIS : A fireman! ANNE *laughs.*

ANTOINE : And then there'll be thirty-six firemen with me.

JEAN-LOUIS : Thirty-six with you?

ANTOINE : Yes, and with me that'll make thirty-seven.

JEAN-LOUIS : And you'll be the chief, eh?

ANTOINE : Yes. But . . . and then you see we have . . . we'll have . . . *He spreads his arms.* . . . two big fire-engines with ladders. *(Still on page 39)*

JEAN-LOUIS : Oh yes. . . .

ANTOINE : Really big ones . . . and, and, and . . . two fire-engines, but they'll be for big fires.

ANNE *laughing*: Oh! . . . I say!

JEAN-LOUIS : Yes? . . . *Still talking to his son.* And if there are little fires, what will you do then?

ANTOINE : What?

JEAN-LOUIS *trying to keep a straight face* : And if there are little fires? . . . What then?

ANTOINE : Oh . . . well, in that case . . . we . . . we won't put up the ladder. That's what we'll do. *The two parents laugh.* But . . . but . . . we'll . . . and then we won't put on much water. That's all. We'll take the axes and we'll . . . bang, and that's it. . . . And then we'll put on water and it'll be all over.*

232. *Medium close-up of* ANNE.

ANNE : Now tell me about *your* job.

Camera pans left to JEAN-LOUIS.

JEAN-LOUIS : Well, you know, my job is a very technical one . . . it's difficult to talk about, women get . . . get bored when one talks about technical matters. All I could tell you are anecdotes, things like . . .

ANNE *off* : Oh no, that doesn't bore me at all.

JEAN-LOUIS : Well, superstition, for instance. You know, racing

---

* End of the fourth reel, about 410 metres.

52

drivers are very superstitious. The number 13 doesn't exist in motor racing.

ANNE *off* : Really?

JEAN-LOUIS : No.

ANNE : You mean, there aren't any cars . . .

JEAN-LOUIS : No car ever carries the number 13 . . . it's the same with other numbers, even. Seventeen — there have been lots of accidents with cars carrying the number 17. In Italy for instance you never have a number 17. The Italians, above all, are very . . . er . . . superstitious. Er, you've heard of . . . Ascari?

The camera pans slowly across to hold ANNE *in medium close-up.*

ANNE : Yes, I think so. . . . Yes, you know . . .

JEAN-LOUIS *off* : He was a racing driver . . . a very great driver, one of the greatest. He got killed a few years ago.

ANNE : Ah, yes, yes, I've heard of him.

JEAN-LOUIS *off* : If Ascari saw a black cat on the track, or even at the side of the track, he stopped.

ANNE *shushes her daughter who is getting restless, off-screen.*

233. Medium close-up of the two of them, JEAN-LOUIS *nearest the camera.*

JEAN-LOUIS : Antoine, tuck in your napkin.

ANNE : We'd better find them something to eat. I think they're hungry.

JEAN-LOUIS *picks up a dish and reaches over to give* FRANÇOISE *and* ANTOINE *some shrimps. Camera pans with the dish.* ANNE *watches him.*

JEAN-LOUIS : Here you are.

ANTOINE *off-screen on the other side of the table* : No . . . I don't like shrimps.

JEAN-LOUIS : You don't like shrimps?

ANTOINE *off* : No.

JEAN-LOUIS *serves* ANNE.

ANNE : Oh . . . thank you.

JEAN-LOUIS : Françoise, don't you want some shrimps?

ANNE *to* FRANÇOISE : What's this? You ate them last Sunday.

JEAN-LOUIS *to* ANTOINE : Do you want some tomatoes?

ANNE *to* FRANÇOISE *who has answered in a whisper* : What?
JEAN-LOUIS : Do you like tomatoes, Antoine?
ANNE *to* FRANÇOISE : What . . . you're not hungry?

Camera pans, losing the adults, as JEAN-LOUIS *reaches across to serve the tomatoes: the two children appear in profile on the right of screen.*

JEAN-LOUIS *off, serving* ANTOINE : I'm not blaming you for not liking shrimps, Antoine, it doesn't matter.
ANNE *off* : But she liked shrimps before.
JEAN-LOUIS *off* : Do you like shrimps?
ANTOINE : No.

234. Medium close-up of JEAN-LOUIS *and* ANNE *laughing, then smiling at each other. A pause.*

JEAN-LOUIS : But these are quite fresh, Antoine.
ANNE *to* FRANÇOISE : Do eat something . . . you can't eat nothing, my pet.

235. High angle medium close-up of ANTOINE, *seated. He rests his chin on the edge of the table.*

ANNE *off* : When you're driving in a race, what do you think about? I mean, what's the most important thing?

236. Close-up of JEAN-LOUIS.

JEAN-LOUIS : Perhaps the sound of the engine. It's so important, even, that I know an engineer who makes exhaust pipes out of organ pipes. It's something which really . . . which you feel going right through your body . . . which . . . which takes hold of you like that. . . .

237. Reverse angle medium shot of the two children seated at table, facing the camera. We see the backs of the two parents in the foreground.

FRANÇOISE : I'm not thirsty either . . . I'm not hungry today . . . I'm sorry.
ANNE : Oh well!
JEAN-LOUIS : Antoine, how do you say Coca-Cola in Spanish?
ANTOINE : Coca-Cola.
JEAN-LOUIS : It's the same as in French then?
ANTOINE *carefully rounding the ' o 's* : No, then you say it Côca-Côla. . . .
JEAN-LOUIS : And how do you say: ' I want some Coca-Cola '?

ANTOINE *proudly* : Quiero Coca-Cola.
The WAITER *appears behind the children and starts to uncork a bottle of wine.*
JEAN-LOUIS : Well, this gentleman is Spanish . . . he doesn't understand. . . . Ask him for a Coca-Cola in Spanish . . . go on, ask him.
238. Close-up of ANNE *smiling.*
JEAN-LOUIS *off* : Do you want some Coca-Cola? If you want some Coca-Cola ask him.
239. Resume on the children. ANTOINE *turns to the* WAITER.
ANTOINE : Coca-Cola para mí!
WAITER : Very good, señor.
ANTOINE : Y para la niña.
The WAITER *pours wine for the parents.*
240. Close-up of ANNE, *laughing.*
241. Close-up of JEAN-LOUIS, *watching the children.*
242. Resume on medium shot of the two children facing the camera, the parents in back view in the foreground.
FRANÇOISE *to her mother* : Can I have some?
ANNE : Of course; wait a moment and we'll get you another glass.
JEAN-LOUIS *to the* WAITER, *off-screen* : Can we have another glass please?
ANTOINE : Dele otro vaso a la niña.
ANNE : How does he come to speak Spanish?
JEAN-LOUIS : He speaks . . . he speaks English as well. Do you know how to ask for another glass in English?
The WAITER *reappears and gives* FRANÇOISE *a glass.*
ANNE *to the* WAITER : Thank you.
ANTOINE : But that man's Spanish.
JEAN-LOUIS : Yes, well, he's Spanish and English. His mother's English and his father's Spanish . . . so you can talk to him in either language.
The WAITER *goes off.*
ANTOINE *stubbornly* : I'd rather talk to him in Span . . . in Spanish.
JEAN-LOUIS : You're quite right.
ANTOINE : Because it's easier.

243. Close-up of Jean-Louis. *He looks towards* Anne *as she speaks, off.*

Anne *off* : After an accident, what's the first thing you think of ?

Jean-Louis : Well, one is angry — yes, it's true, one is angry . . . hm . . . it's stupid . . . but you're angry. You see, when one has an accident it's usually . . . well, it's one's own fault . . . it's because one takes a bend too fast. For instance, you take a bend at 140 kilometres an hour. If you take it at 141 you go off the track. . . . If you take it at 139 you lose the race . . . so you have to find the exact limit every time.

244. Resume on medium shot, the children facing us, the parents backs to the camera in the foreground.

Jean-Louis : Say : ' I love you ' in Spanish . . . to Françoise.

245. Close-up of Anne, *smiling indulgently.*

Antoine *off* : To who ?

Jean-Louis *off* : To Françoise.

246. Resume on medium shot.

Antoine *turning to* Françoise : Te quiero.

247. Reverse angle medium close-up, the parents facing the camera. Jean-Louis *writes something on a cigarette packet, then leans towards* Anne. *(Still on page 39) She reads it and smiles.*

Jean-Louis : In real life, when something isn't serious one says : it's just like the movies. Why do you think one doesn't take the cinema seriously ?

Anne *smiling* : Oh, I don't know . . . perhaps because one only goes when everything is all right.

Jean-Louis : Do you think one should go when things are going wrong, then ?

Anne : Why not ?

248. Medium shot of the children. Antoine *is playing with his fork as if it were an aeroplane or a rocket.*

Antoine : It's . . . it's taken off . . . the aeroplane's taken off.

The fork falls onto a plate with a clatter.

249. Medium close-up of the two parents: Jean-Louis *is in the foreground, in profile,* Anne *beside him, turned*

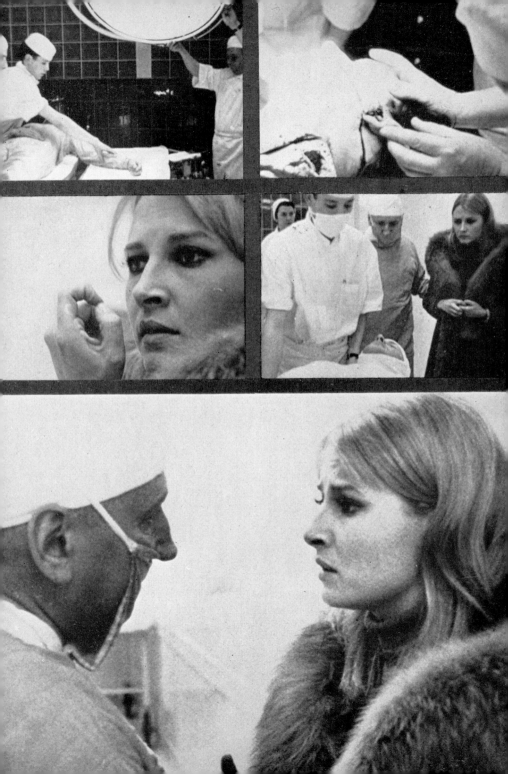

towards him and facing the camera. The WAITER *bends over them.*

WAITER : May I clear the table, sir?

JEAN-LOUIS : Yes, please.

JEAN-LOUIS *takes a cigarette, cuts it in half and lights one half with his lighter. The flame is enormous.*

ANNE *who is also smoking* : Why do you cut up your cigarettes?

JEAN-LOUIS : To smoke less.

ANNE : You could just smoke one less each time. . . .

JEAN-LOUIS : That's true. . . . Antoine has told me that already.

250. High angle medium close-up of ANTOINE *looking bored.*

JEAN-LOUIS *continues off* : But tell me, have you ever thought . . .

251. Resume on the two adults.

JEAN-LOUIS : . . . of being an actress too?

ANNE : Yes, but you know I would have found it very boring.

JEAN-LOUIS : Why?

ANNE : I don't know. Because . . . one rather has to . . . I really don't know, one has to . . . *She laughs, slightly embarrassed.*

JEAN-LOUIS : After all, playing in comedy isn't very difficult, is it? . . . No more difficult than being a continuity girl or a film editor, surely?

ANNE *laughing* : Oh yes?

JEAN-LOUIS : I think . . . well, I don't know, it's not my field.

ANNE : But what do you think? You're a spectator after all. What do you think?

JEAN-LOUIS : Oh, I don't know. I don't think it's . . . it's not very difficult, it's the . . .

ANNE : It's not a question of being . . . of whether it's difficult or not . . . it's just that everyone has his own métier, don't you think?

JEAN-LOUIS : No, but if one's good-looking . . . I don't know. I wouldn't have thought it was very difficult to play in comedy. It's the director who makes the film, isn't it?

ANNE : Yes, but why haven't you tried being an actor? You're good-looking.

They both burst out laughing. A pause.

JEAN-LOUIS : No, because, I don't know . . . I've never thought of it. But if I worked in films, rather than be a technician . . . I don't know, I think I'd probably prefer to be an actor.

ANNE : No . . . I must say, I'm very happy doing the job I do. *She pushes back a lock of hair.* No, I don't think I would have liked being an actress.

JEAN-LOUIS : There's more to being a technician. It's more of a profession. . . .

ANNE : It's not that there's more to it. Perhaps it's more real. . . .

A pause, they look at each other and laugh.

JEAN-LOUIS : Yes. You know, there's a whole heap of questions . . . I . . . I'm very fond of . . . I go to the cinema a lot. . . . There are heaps of questions I would like to ask you.

252. Close-up of JEAN-LOUIS' left hand, wearing a wedding ring, resting on the back of ANNE'S chair, very close to her arm. (Still on page 39)

253. Resume on medium close-up of the two of them.

ANNE : But you seem to be very well informed about the cinema.

JEAN-LOUIS : No, I've got a vague idea of what goes on, like everyone else. I read one or two film magazines. I pick up a bit from them.

ANNE : Yes, but you know I'm not really . . . I haven't really been in films very . . . a very long time. I haven't worked much with the old hands.

254. Close-up of JEAN-LOUIS' hand on the back of ANNE'S chair.

JEAN-LOUIS *off* : Tell me some more . . .

255. Resume on the two of them.

JEAN-LOUIS : . . . about actors and actresses, that kind of thing.

ANNE : Does that really interest you all that much?

256. Reverse angle medium close-up as the camera pans right and holds on the two children.

ANTOINE *to* FRANÇOISE, *in English* : You are a little girl and

66

you are a big little, big . . .

257. *Close-up of* ANNE *smiling.*

ANTOINE *off* : . . . big girl and you are a big boy . . . and you . . . are . . . a big . . .

258. *Resume on the children. (Still on page 39)*

ANTOINE *pointing at* JEAN-LOUIS *and then at himself* : . . . boy and you are a big boy . . .

259. *Close-up of* ANNE *looking on tenderly,* JEAN-LOUIS *partly visible in the foreground.*

JEAN-LOUIS : Big boy . . . no! Have you had a good meal? *To* ANNE. Have you eaten enough?

ANNE : Yes . . . but I'd like some coffee.

JEAN-LOUIS *calling to the* WAITER : One coffee, please. . . . ANTOINE *continues to babble in English, off.* ANNE *turns to watch.*

JEAN-LOUIS : Be quiet, Antoine . . . be quiet. . . . Come on Antoine, be quiet now. What do you want to do now?

FRANÇOISE *off* : I don't want to do anything. . . . He just wants to play.

FRANÇOISE *and* ANTOINE : Yes, yes, yes . . . a boat trip . . .

260. *Medium close-up of the two children grinning delightedly across the table.*

FRANÇOISE *and* ANTOINE : Yes, yes, yes . . . a boat trip . . . a boat trip!

ANNE *off* : Don't you think it's a little cold?

261. *Close-up of* ANNE *smiling. She drains her glass.*

JEAN-LOUIS *off* : I promised, remember? I promised.

ANTOINE *off* : Yes . . . yes, yes.

JEAN-LOUIS : Have you been good? Have you been good the whole week . . . do you swear?

262. *Medium close-up of the two children, facing the camera across the table, both bubbling over with excitement.*

FRANÇOISE : Oh, yes, yes, he's been very good . . . yes, yes.

ANTOINE : Yes, yes!

263. *Close-up of* ANNE *smiling, leaning her chin on her hand.*

JEAN-LOUIS *to* FRANÇOISE *off* : And you . . . have you been good too?

67

FRANÇOISE *off* : Yes.
264. Resume on the two children, overjoyed.
JEAN-LOUIS *off* : Okay . . . shall we go for a boat trip? . . .
Come on, we're off.
The two children leap to their feet.
ANNE *off* : Hurry then . . . go and get your coats.
Pan to follow the children as they rush towards the cloak-room, then hold on the parents, still seated at the table:
JEAN-LOUIS *is in the foreground in three-quarter back view, his hand resting on the back of* ANNE'S *chair. She is facing camera.*
ANNE : Do you think we'll be able to get on a boat?
265. Music. Close-up of JEAN-LOUIS' *hand on the back of* ANNE'S *chair. He removes it.**

266. The music continues. Exterior shot in normal colour. The camera tracks sideways, following a fishing boat in medium shot as it passes behind the piles of the jetty, making for the open sea. ANNE *and* JEAN-LOUIS *can be seen standing on the deck. (Still on page 40)*
267. Slightly high angle medium shot of JEAN-LOUIS *on the boat, crouching down between the two children.* ANNE *is standing in front of the camera, out of focus.*
268. Reverse angle medium close-up of ANNE *as seen by* JEAN-LOUIS, *standing in the stern of the boat as it moves along the harbour. (Still on page 40)*
269. High angle medium close-up of JEAN-LOUIS *crouched beside* ANTOINE. ANNE *and* FRANÇOISE *stand in the background.*
270. Low angle medium close-up of JEAN-LOUIS *looking up, talking to* ANNE *off-screen.* ANTOINE *is in the foreground.*
271. High angle medium close-up of ANNE *looking out over the stern, silhouetted against the sunlit water, her hair flying in the breeze. Camera tilts down to include* FRANÇOISE *as* ANNE *puts an arm round her.*
272. Low angle medium close-up of the four of them in

---

* End of the fifth reel, 410 metres.

68

the stern of the boat, laughing happily as the harbour is left behind.

273. Close-up of ANNE *bending over* FRANÇOISE, *smiling, her hair blowing around her face.*

274. Medium shot of the side of the fishing boat, hung with fenders, churning through the water. The music continues.

275. Close-up of ANNE, *windswept and smiling.*

276. Low angle medium close-up of JEAN-LOUIS *looking up at her, both of them hanging onto a boom.*

277. Medium close-up of JEAN-LOUIS, *who has taken off his overcoat, gazing seriously at* ANNE, *who is in back view in the foreground.*

278. Reverse shot of ANNE *looking at him. She drops her gaze.*

279. High angle close-up of ANTOINE *in back view, hanging on to* JEAN-LOUIS' *hand.*

280. High angle medium close-up of JEAN-LOUIS *speaking in* ANNE'S *ear, leaning over the two children.*

281. A slightly closer shot of the same scene.

282. Medium shot. ANNE *opens her coat to shelter* JEAN-LOUIS *as he lights a cigarette. Tilt down to show the two children in the foreground, looking slightly nervously over the side of the boat.*

283. Close-up of JEAN-LOUIS *puffing at his cigarette. Pan to show* ANNE *in profile.*

284. Medium close-up of the two of them, looking out over the side. The boatman can be seen in the background.

285. High angle close-up of JEAN-LOUIS *talking to* FRANÇOISE. *The music continues.*

286. Close-up of the two parents on the tossing boat. JEAN-LOUIS *momentarily puts an arm round* ANNE.

287. Low angle close-up of JEAN-LOUIS *as he nuzzles* FRANÇOISE'S *cheek.* ANNE *is in the background.*

288. Close-up of FRANÇOISE. JEAN-LOUIS' *hand caresses her face.*

289. Medium close-up of the two adults. JEAN-LOUIS *says something in* ANNE'S *ear. They both laugh happily and bend down to the children.*

290. High angle close-up of the two children huddled together in JEAN-LOUIS' *overcoat, which he is holding tightly round them.* ANNE *lays a hand on* JEAN-LOUIS' *arm as they bend down over the children.*

291. High angle medium close-up of the foam breaking away under the fishing boat's bows.

292. Long shot, tracking across the sunlit water, the fishing boat pitching in the distance.

293. Close-up of JEAN-LOUIS *and* ANNE *in profile. She bends forward as he brushes her hair from her face. (Still on page 40) They smile at each other.*

294. High angle medium shot of the two of them in the bows of the boat as it re-enters the harbour. The two children stand between them, huddled in JEAN-LOUIS' *overcoat.*

295. Close-up of the children huddled in the coat, looking cold and anxious. JEAN-LOUIS' *hand caresses* ANTOINE'S *nose, then reaches towards* ANNE'S *hand, wearing her wedding ring (Still on page 40), hesitates and withdraws.*

296. Medium long shot of the boat tied up at the quay: a sailor helps the children jump off the boat. ANTOINE, *with renewed confidence now he is back on dry land, takes* FRANÇOISE *by the hand, and the two children come towards camera. (Still on page 40)*

297. Medium shot of sunlit waves breaking on the sandy shore.

298. Long shot of the beach, looking out to sea: camera tracks slowly as the two parents walk along the shore while the children run to and fro laughing. The music ends and we hear the roar of the waves and the cries of the seagulls as they swoop across the picture. The sea is grey-green beneath an overcast sky. The track loses ANNE *as* JEAN-LOUIS *runs after the children, trying to trip them up.* FRANÇOISE *escapes, but* ANTOINE *sprawls in the sand (Stills on page 57) and* JEAN-LOUIS *gathers him up immediately in his arms.* ANNE *runs up to join them. . . . Then* JEAN-LOUIS *puts down* ANTOINE *who rushes off to join* FRANÇOISE. *A ferry boat passes in the back-ground, sounding its siren. The track ends as the children rush towards the sea and camera zooms back to widen the field of view. We hear the parents talking as they walk along side by side.*

ANNE : The children are really happy.

JEAN-LOUIS : They get on well with each other, don't they? . . . They've been friends for a long time. *Camera continues to zoom back slowly to a very long shot.* Antoine told me he'd noticed Françoise a long time ago . . . and thought she was very pretty . . . but he'd only spoken to her twice.

ANNE : How sweet.

The music begins again. There follows a series of brief shots taken in and around Deauville.

299. The boat with the jetty and lighthouse in the back-ground.

300. A roadsign marked DIVERSION.

301. The roadsign stuck in a pile of sand at a crossroads.

302. Some ponies in an enclosure.

303. Houses on the side of a hill, lit by the setting sun.

304. The Casino with a statue in the foreground.

305. A building site, the Casino in the background.

306. A boarded-up nightclub by the building site.

307. Long shot of the wooden promenade. The tide is out and the sun is low. Camera tracks after an old man walking his dog along the promenade.

ANNE *off* : What a marvellous sight . . . that man with his dog. . . . Look . . . they both walk in the same way.

308. Medium shot of the same scene. The man shambles away from camera with the dog, shot through a telephoto lens. (Still on page 57)

JEAN-LOUIS *off* : You're right. *A pause.* Have you heard of the sculptor Giacometti?

309. Reverse angle shot. The man comes towards camera, now no more than a dark silhouette against the light of the setting sun, which floods the screen.

ANNE *off* : Oh, yes. I think he's wonderful.

JEAN-LOUIS *off* : Do you know, he once said something remarkable. . . . He said : ' In a fire . . . if I had to choose

71

between a Rembrandt and a cat . . . I'd save the cat.'
ANNE *off* : Yes, and he also said : ' I would let the cat go afterwards.'
JEAN-LOUIS *off* : Really?
ANNE *off* : Oh yes! That's just what's so marvellous about it, don't you think?
JEAN-LOUIS *off* : Yes, that's perfect. That means : ' Between art and life, I choose life.'
ANNE *off* : It's marvellous.

The MAN *comes right up to camera, which pans across to the waves breaking on the sandy shore. As they continue to talk, off, we see a series of shots of the town as night falls.*
310. Medium shot of a bulldozer turning in the crossroads near the building site. The music, which has continued softly throughout the preceding scene, gets louder.
ANNE *off* : Why did you ask me that?
311. Long shot of the harbour wall with the town behind.
JEAN-LOUIS *off* : About Giacometti?
312. Long shot of buildings across the water, silhouetted against the evening sky.
ANNE *off* : Yes.
313. Forward tracking shot from a car moving along by the harbour wall, as darkness falls.
JEAN-LOUIS : Because of . . . that man with his dog.

314. Blue filter. Close-up of ANNE *from the side, in the passenger seat of the Mustang at night. She smiles across at* JEAN-LOUIS. *The music continues.*
315. Similar close-up of JEAN-LOUIS *driving. He turns towards* ANNE *a couple of times, smiling also.*
316. Medium close-up, from behind, of JEAN-LOUIS' *hand on the wheel. We can also see the dashboard and the windscreen. Outside it is raining and the wipers are going. Camera follows* JEAN-LOUIS' *hand as he changes gear, hesitates, then places it tenderly over* ANNE'S. *(Still on page 57)*
317. Close-up of ANNE *in profile, overcoming her emotion and suddenly assuming a cold, severe expression. (Still on*

page 57) She looks from her hand to JEAN-LOUIS' *several times, and turns towards the window. After a time she looks at him again.*

ANNE : You've never told me anything about your wife.

318. Medium close-up of JEAN-LOUIS, *in profile, his eyes fixed on the road. He glances at* ANNE *a couple of times, looking sad and uneasy. The music ends.*

. . . .

319. Flashback, normal colour. We are in JEAN-LOUIS' *apartment. Medium close-up of* VALERIE, JEAN-LOUIS' *wife, facing the camera as she speaks on the telephone.*

VALERIE : [Hello, darling, how are you? You're nervous . . . really? I'm not at all . . . I'm going to watch the start on television. Yes, yes, number 12? Yes, I'll be following you all the time. Yes, I'm taking Antoine to my mother's tomorrow. Yes, I'll be there tomorrow at the finish. No, no, I'm all right, and anyway . . . *Noise of an aeroplane.* Yes; oh no, no really.*] You know I'll be with you all the time, at every second, right to the end. I love you, Jean-Louis, I love you.

The flashback continues. The next sequence, showing the start of the Le Mans 24 hours race, is shot in black and white through a sepia filter.
320. Close-up of JEAN-LOUIS' *tense face. Background noise of engines being revved etc. before the start of the race.*
321–325. A series of five low angle shots of cars being rolled forward to the starting line.
326. Resume on JEAN-LOUIS' *face. He glances down nervously at his watch.*
327. Low angle shot of another car with a Paris registration number being rolled forward by mechanics.
328. JEAN-LOUIS *glances down at his watch again.*
329. Close-up of his hand drawing back his sleeve to look at his watch. He is dressed in driver's overalls, and carrying a crash-helmet.
330. Low angle medium close-up of a clock at the side

---

* The whole of the first part of this conversation, in brackets, was cut in the final editing.

of the circuit, showing seven minutes to four, and bearing the legend DUTRAY — LE MANS.

331–336. Another series of six shots showing cars being rolled to their starting positions. Engines roar, a voice talks continuously over a loudspeaker.

337. Medium shot. Camera circles round a group of drivers waiting for the start.

338. Similar shot of a vast AMERICAN *festooned with cameras, photographing the scene.*

339. Close-up of JEAN-LOUIS' *face. He glances downwards again as a voice is heard from the loudspeaker off. It continues through the next few shots.*

LOUDSPEAKER *off* : Engines may not under any circumstances be started until all engines have completely stopped. Is that understood?

340. High angle close-up of JEAN-LOUIS' *hands as he starts to put on his gloves.*

341. Long shot of the track, the cars lined up diagonally on the left, the white circles marking the drivers' positions on the right.

342. Very low angle medium shot of a RACING DRIVER *(clearly not in the race) signing autographs.*

LOUDSPEAKER *off* : Will you please go to your starting positions.

343. High angle medium shot panning with a DRIVER *as he moves to his starting position, fastening his helmet.*

344. Close-up of JEAN-LOUIS' *face as he starts to move.*

LOUDSPEAKER *off* : The tricolour flag is carried by two scouts. Bravo! May we have the track cleared completely, please. . . .

345. Close-up of JEAN-LOUIS' *gloved hand carrying his helmet, camera moving with him as he walks across the track.*

346. Resume on his face as he walks, frowning with tension.

347. High angle medium close-up of his legs as he arrives at his starting position — number 12.

348. High angle long shot of the start, three officials standing in the centre of shot with the tricolour flag. (Still on page 58)

LOUDSPEAKER *off* : The start will be in one minute. . . .

349. Medium close-up of an American DRIVER *in his starting position, chewing gum.*

350. Medium close-up of two youthful spectators, one with binoculars.

351. Resume on the American DRIVER. *He glances at his watch.*

352. Low angle close-up of the circuit clock showing one minute to four.

353. Low angle medium close-up of JEAN-LOUIS *putting on his helmet. (Still on page 58)*

LOUDSPEAKER *off* : He's unfurling the tricolour flag . . .

354. Long shot of the officials in the middle of the track (as 348). One of them slowly raises the flag.

LOUDSPEAKER *off* : . . . thirty seconds to go . . .

355. High angle long shot of the drivers lined up for the start, the American in the foreground.

356. Low angle close-up of JEAN-LOUIS, *now wearing glasses. He stands tensely, ready to run. The chatter of the expectant crowd is heard off.*

357. Resume on long shot of the drivers (as 355).

358. Reverse angle long shot of the drivers crouching forward, ready to sprint for their cars. (Still on page 58)

359. Another long shot (as 357).

LOUDSPEAKER *off* : Attention please . . .

360. Extreme close-up of JEAN-LOUIS' *tense face. The crowd falls silent.*

LOUDSPEAKER *off* : . . . four seconds . . .

361. Low angle medium close-up of the circuit clock as it clicks on to four o'clock precisely.

362. High angle long shot of the three officials standing in the middle of the track. The flag drops. The crowd roars, and the drivers sprint across the track and leap into their cars.

363. Medium close-up of JEAN-LOUIS, *seen through the window of his car, as he leaps in and slams the door.*

364. Resume on long shot (as 362). The engines start with a roar.

365. Reverse angle long shot as the cars leap forward, JEAN-LOUIS' *car, number 12, nearest camera.*

366. Reverse shot: with an ear-splitting noise, the cars accelerate away from the start, wheels spinning as they turn. (Still on page 58)

367. Long shot of the cars streaking up the straight, away from camera, photographers crouched at the track side.

368. Similar shot, reverse angle.

369. Long shot as they come round a curve. The howl of the engines gets louder and camera zooms back as they sweep by in a cloud of dust and exhaust smoke.

370. Cut to JEAN-LOUIS *and* VALERIE'S *apartment, still in sepia. We see the back of* VALERIE'S *head in close-up as she sits watching the start of the race on television.*

COMMENTATOR *off*: . . . are now on the first lap. There is absolutely nothing to say yet about this race, which promises to be extremely exciting . . .

371. Reverse angle close-up of VALERIE, *facing camera, smoking, as she nervously watches the television screen. (Still on page 58)*

COMMENTATOR *off*: . . . All I can tell you is that millions of viewers are now watching it with us on Eurovision and will, of course, be doing so for the next twenty-four hours. You'll be hearing from me again this evening at ten o'clock, and I think that by then, still on Eurovision, of course, the race will already have begun to take shape. Until then . . . *Fade out.*

372. Long shot of the circuit at night, still in sepia. An ambulance speeds along inside the track, the sound of its siren mingling with the roar of the cars and the voice of a COMMENTATOR *off. Camera pans with it as it comes to a stop near a Dunlop sign.*

373. Medium shot: attendants, wearing reflective jackets with a red cross on the back, lay a body gently on the ground near an overturned car.

374. Medium shot of the attendants lifting the body on a stretcher and carrying it to the ambulance. The noise of the siren continues.

375. Medium shot of surgeons, assistants and nurses preparing for an operation in the operating theatre at the Le Mans hospital. Camera pans as a stretcher bearing JEAN-LOUIS' *body is rolled past towards the operating*

table. Noise of engines as cars pass on the circuit outside. Track in as the nurses lift JEAN-LOUIS' *body, still clad in Ford overalls, onto the operating table. (Still on page 59)*
376. Medium close-up of his lifeless face. A SURGEON *turns* JEAN-LOUIS' *head to show rivulets of blood coming from his ear and neck. (Still on page 59) Camera tilts up to show the face of the* SURGEON *and assistants looking down from above.*
377–379. A series of three similar shots, camera panning swiftly right to show the cars on the circuit in high angle shot as they sweep past the pits at night, engines howling, headlamps ablaze.
380. Low angle medium shot of commentators or officials at the track side.
381. Another panning shot as a car sweeps past.
382. Close-up of VALERIE *driving feverishly, seen through the windscreen of her car. The picture is still sepia.*

COMMENTATOR *on the car radio, off* : The Ferraris are now leading. You will have already heard that the driver, Jean-Louis Duroc, has just had an accident. Only a few minutes ago in fact, to the right of the stands. . . . It looks like an extremely serious one, too . . . as Jean-Louis Duroc has been rushed to the hospital block on the Le Mans circuit.

383. Close-up of a sign lit by car headlights: LE MANS 24 HOURS MOTOR RACE.

COMMENTATOR *continuing off* : He has still not regained consciousness. We will, of course, keep you informed of his condition. At the moment all we know is that he is on the operating table.

384. Close-up of the hands of the surgeons operating on JEAN-LOUIS.
385. A shot of the corridor outside the operating theatre. VALERIE'S *legs, wearing boots, are seen in medium close-up, as she walks up and down.*
386. Close-up of her leaning her forehead against the white wall of the corridor.
387. Low angle medium shot of the corridor: a NURSE *runs past* VALERIE, *who stands looking anxiously after her.*

388. Medium close-up of VALERIE *from behind, walking away from camera, hands clasping her leather handbag behind her back.*

389. Close-up of her in profile: she is sitting down, a lighted cigarette in her hand, trying not to bite her nails.

390. Low angle medium close-up of her squatting on the floor in the corridor, nervously biting her fingers as two doctors pass by.

391. Close-up of VALERIE. *She watches with increasing agitation as assistants and nurses pass to and fro without paying her any attention. (Still on page 59) She looks anxiously along the corridor and gets up.*

392. Long shot of the corridor, with some nurses standing at the far end.

393. Low angle medium close-up of VALERIE, *her forehead pressed against the wall.*

394. Close-up as she leans her head back hopelessly.

395. Medium close-up as she looks round with increasing agitation. Some nurses stand talking in the background.

396. Medium close-up of her elbow resting tensely on her hand.

397. Medium close-up of her from behind, walking along, leaning against the wall. Pan left, following her gaze to the door of the operating theatre, which is closed.

398. Low angle medium close-up of her squatting on the floor again, her hand pressed to her mouth.*

399. Music. Medium shot of VALERIE *still waiting in the corridor. The door of the operating theatre finally opens. Panic-stricken,* VALERIE *presses herself against the wall as an* ASSISTANT *emerges with a trolley bearing* JEAN-LOUIS' *body, followed by several nurses. The trolley rolls towards camera, which tracks slowly backwards, and tilts down to show* JEAN-LOUIS' *head, almost completely hidden by bandages. In the background,* VALERIE *staggers after the little convoy. The* SURGEON *comes up to her and takes her by the arm, holding her back. (Still on page 59)*

---

* End of the sixth reel, 405 metres.

78

Camera tilts up, losing the stretcher. VALERIE *looks haggard, with staring eyes and open mouth. She listens in increasing agitation as the* SURGEON *talks to her. We do not hear his words. The voice of the* RADIO COMMENTATOR *cuts in.*

COMMENTATOR *off*: Eight o'clock in the morning and the infernal round continues without any change. Three Ferraris leading. During the night, which has been a particularly dramatic one, there has been a continuous succession of mechanical failures . . . and over fifty per cent of the starters are now out of the race, including, of course, Jean-Louis Duroc . . . Jean-Louis Duroc, whose dramatic fate we have all been following.

400. Medium long shot of VALERIE *and the* SURGEON *in the corridor. Camera tracks in on the two of them, and* VALERIE *becomes increasingly agitated as the* SURGEON *tells her of* JEAN-LOUIS' *condition. Hardly able to stand, she leans against the wall and weeps. The* SURGEON *vainly tries to calm her.*

COMMENTATOR *continuing, off*: As you know, he was in the operating theatre for three hours. But you will not know that while Jean-Louis Duroc remains in a coma another drama has taken place, a drama which concerns him intimately. In fact . . . but here I must break off for a moment as I see Graham Hill coming into re-fuel — Graham Hill who is still in the race and still has a chance of winning. . . . As I was saying, a drama has taken place in the very corridors of the hospital, outside the operating theatre.

401. Medium close-up of the two of them. (Still on page 59) Suddenly VALERIE *tears away from the* SURGEON *and rushes madly towards camera, knocking into a* NURSE *on the way.*

COMMENTATOR *continuing, off*: Jean-Louis Duroc's wife arrived at the hospital last night and was informed by the doctors themselves of her husband's extremely serious condition.

402. As the COMMENTATOR *continues, fast panning shot following a car on the Le Mans circuit in the early morning.*

79

403. High angle shot of the vast Le Mans car park in the early morning, taken from an aircraft.
404. Another similar shot.

COMMENTATOR *continuing, off* : And then a most terrible, horrifying thing happened. Already worn out by the tension of the race and her husband's accident, Madame Duroc broke down completely.

405. Fast panning shot as a car streaks under the Dunlop bridge; camera holds on an abandoned car at the side of the track.
406. A slightly longer panning shot as another car passes.
407. As the COMMENTATOR *finishes, medium close-up of a television screen showing the race, the TV camera panning with a particular car. At the bottom of the screen a digital counter shows the lap times, the tenths of a second ticking rapidly by.*

COMMENTATOR *continuing, off* : . . . and it has just leaked out . . . that Madame Duroc committed suicide. We don't know yet under what circumstances.
End of flashback.

. . . .

408. Resume on the Mustang at night; black and white with a yellowish filter. Medium close-up of the windscreen from outside, drenched in rain, the wipers in action. The car is stationary. Camera pans slowly across to ANNE, *looking anguished.* JEAN-LOUIS' *hand caresses her cheek.*
409. Medium close-up of JEAN-LOUIS, *through the windscreen. He glances out of the side window. There is silence, except for the noise of the rain and the windscreen wipers.*
410. Resume on ANNE. *She finally turns to* JEAN-LOUIS.
411. Medium close-up of the two of them through the side window, JEAN-LOUIS *facing camera,* ANNE *in profile in the foreground.*

JEAN-LOUIS : I shan't be around this week. I'll be driving in the Monte Carlo Rally. But as soon as I get back . . . *He smiles briefly.* . . . Montmartre 15-40.
ANNE *leaning forward* : Well. Goodnight.
JEAN-LOUIS : Goodnight.
She steps out onto the pavement and goes out of frame.

80

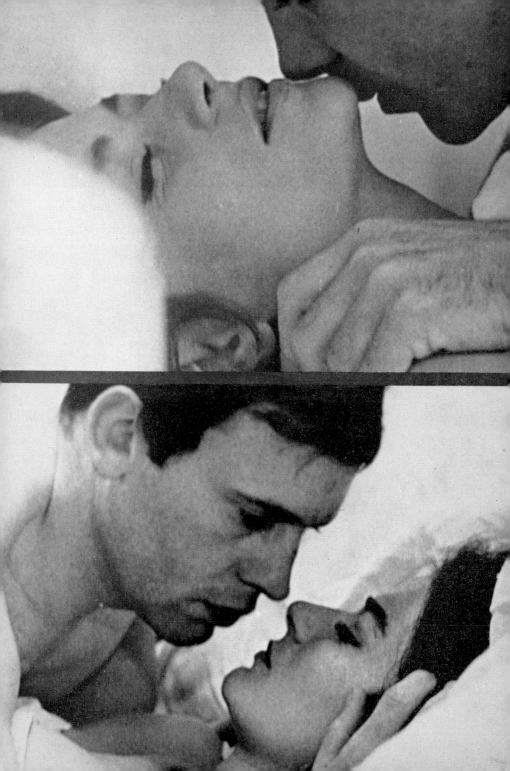

Jean-Louis *shuts the door and drives off straight away, camera panning briefly with the car.*
412. *Close-up of her, standing in the doorway of the apartment house, watching him go. She looks pensive for a moment, then turns and opens the door.*

The next sequence takes place in Jean-Louis' *apartment, or perhaps that of his mistress* Yane, *still black and white with yellow filter.*
413. *Black screen, then a door opens and* Jean-Louis, *his back to the camera, enters the bedroom, taking off his coat. Camera pans as he goes over to the bed where a young woman,* Yane, *is dozing. He turns on the bedside lamp and the woman wakes up. We see the two of them in medium shot.*
Yane : What time is it?
Jean-Louis *looks at his watch and sits down beside her on the bed. She remains lying down.*
Jean-Louis : Five past one.
Yane : Did you have a good trip? How's the little boy?
Jean-Louis : Fine.
Yane : And you?
Jean-Louis : Fine. *A pause.* I've got some bad news for you.
She raises her head slightly and looks at him.
Yane : You didn't find me a secretaire? You can't have looked properly.
Jean-Louis *embarrassed* : Oh no, I assure you . . . I went to all the antique shops in Deauville . . . but no one had a Louis XV secretaire.
Yane : Never mind. *A pause.* Aren't you going to get undressed?
Jean-Louis : That's just what I'm doing.
He gets up and camera pans right round as he goes out of the door and along the corridor into the bathroom. He takes off his jacket.
Yane *off* : When are you going to introduce me to your son?
Jean-Louis : When he's old enough to seduce you.
Yane *off* : I'd make a good mother, you know.
Jean-Louis : Yes . . . I know.

YANE *off* : Hey, I see you're going out with twins now.
Pan back again as JEAN-LOUIS *comes back into the
bedroom, unbuttoning his shirt-collar.* YANE *is still lying
in bed.*
JEAN-LOUIS : Who told you that?
YANE : ' The Auto ' . . . the Auto thing . . . there.
Pan further as JEAN-LOUIS *goes and picks up a magazine
from an armchair beside the bed.*
JEAN-LOUIS : ' Sport Auto '?
YANE : Yes.
*He sits down in the armchair and leafs through the
magazine.*
JEAN-LOUIS : What page?
YANE : Twenty-nine.
JEAN-LOUIS : You're right.
414. Medium shot, normal colour, of JEAN-LOUIS *and
his co-driver standing on either side of a sports-racing car,
with two attractive and identically dressed girls between
them.*
415. Resume on the room; black and white, yellow filter.
JEAN-LOUIS : You didn't read it all. Listen . . . ' Today the
racing driver, Jean-Louis Duroc, met a young Parisienne in
Deauville. *He pauses for a moment, improvising.* They spent
the afternoon together. They had lunch together . . . and
they drove four hundred kilometres, still together. . . . They
parted half an hour ago.'
YANE *propping herself up on her elbow* : Why are you telling
me all this?
JEAN-LOUIS : Because it's true . . . ' Sport Auto ' always tells
the truth.

*The scene changes to the start of the Monte Carlo Rally
at Rheims. All the shots of the rally up to the finish are
taken in black and white through a pinkish sepia filter.*
*416. Medium close-up of a musician of the Garde
Républicaine clashing a pair of cymbals. Loud, brassy
music, slightly out of tune.*
417. Medium shot of the brass band, the CONDUCTOR
beating time, in back view in the foreground.

418. High angle medium shot of the drummers in the band. Behind them the buglers raise their instruments with a flourish.

419. Resume on the CYMBAL PLAYER.

420. High angle medium close-up of a DRUMMER. *The music continues loudly.*

421. Close-up of his drum as he plays.

422. Medium shot of the CONDUCTOR *in back view.*

423. Medium close-up of one of the musicians, brass instruments and music stands all round him.

424. Another similar shot.

425. Medium shot of crash-helmeted motor-cycle police lined up at the starting point. The voice of a COMMENTATOR *is heard and continues over the next series of shots.*

COMMENTATOR *off* : This is Rheims . . . Rheims, international capital of champagne and, for this evening, world capital of motoring for the start of the 35th Monte Carlo Rally. . . . Considering the adverse weather conditions, which you are no doubt familiar with already, it looks as though this will be one of the hardest runs yet.

426. Low angle medium close-up of a car as it sets off at a signal from the marshals. Pan to medium close-up of the wheels.

427. Medium close-up and pan with a Citroen DS as it sets off in its turn.

428. Low angle medium close-up of another DRIVER *in his car, being given a count-down by a* MARSHAL.

429. Close-up of the back of a Lancia bearing a plate carrying the legend MONTE CARLO RALLY 1966. *Tilt up as it moves away.*

430. High angle medium shot of another car moving off, headlamps ablaze, preceded by a motor-cycle.

COMMENTATOR *continuing, off* : As I am speaking to you now, other competitors are leaving Oslo, Minsk, London, Athens, Lisbon and Hamburg.

431. Low angle medium close-up of another car moving off.

432. High angle medium shot of a CAMERAMAN *filming a Mini-Cooper bearing the number 168. Pan with the*

car as it moves off down the slope from the start.
433. Medium close-up of JEAN-LOUIS *in conversation with an* OFFICIAL.
434. Another similar shot.
COMMENTATOR *continuing, off*: There are 273 of them altogether . . . and amongst these, of course, is Jean-Louis Duroc, whose Mustang number 184 is stopping in front of us at the moment . . .*
435. Low angle medium close-up of the side of the Mustang, the driver's door open.
436. Low angle medium shot of the Mustang, waiting for the signal to start.
COMMENTATOR *off*:. . . and will be setting off in a few seconds from now. Jean-Louis Duroc will be sharing the driving with his team-mate Chemin. . . .**
437. Low angle medium close-up of the car as a MAR-SHAL *gives the count-down. Pan with the car as it moves off to loud cheers,* CHEMIN *grinning through the driver's window.*
438. Close-up of JEAN-LOUIS *from behind in the passenger seat. (Still on page 60) He grins across at* CHEMIN, *off-screen, as the car roars off into the night.*
439. Theme music. Low angle long shot of cars' headlamps appearing over the horizon and moving past camera.
440. Fast panning shot from inside another car, camera moving with the Mustang as it comes up behind and sweeps past, going off into the distance.
441. Low angle panning shot of the front of the Mustang, all its lights blazing.
442. Another panning shot, with dazzle effect from the headlamps as the car sweeps along a road.
443. Normal colour. Medium shot from inside a Paris newspaper kiosk, in the daytime. ANNE *is buying ' France-*

---

* Although the French dialogue transcript gives the car's number as 184, and the white Mustang seen at Montlhéry in an earlier sequence also carried this number, the car in which JEAN-LOUIS and CHEMIN move off in fact bears the number 145.
** Jean-Louis Trintignant has, in fact, driven in the Monte Carlo Rally. ' Chemin ' is Henri Chemin, competitions director for Ford-France.

soir' and 'L'Equipe' and one or two other motoring journals. (Still on page 60)
444. Medium close-up, tracking out in front of her as she walks along the street reading 'L'Equipe'.
445. Reverse shot of the paper, over her shoulder. A headline reads: 'Confidence reigns in the Ford team.'
446. Return to sepia. Long shot of a hairpin bend. The Mustang passes, camera panning as it swerves round.
447–449. Three similar shots of cars rounding hairpin bends, camera swinging to follow them, accompanied by the roar of engines and the scream of tyres. First a Mini-Cooper moving away from camera, then a Ford Cortina and Lancia Flavia, both coming towards it.
450. Colour: Long shot of four camels standing majestically in the middle of a desert. (Still on page 60)
451–452. Sepia: Another bend taken at high speed, first by a Renault, then by the Cortina.
453. Colour: Medium shot of the camels moving along, now with riders. The music continues loudly.
454–456. Sepia: Three more shots of cars rounding another bend, tyres screaming: a Porsche, the Lancia, then a Citroen ID with its front wing torn off.
457. Colour: Low angle close-up of a camel's head, the RIDER behind.
458. Sepia: Medium shot from road level as another Cortina rounds a bend.
459. Colour: High angle close-up of floodlights on the desert sand. They light up.
460. Sepia: Medium shot of a Rover 2000 speeding round a blind corner away from camera.
461. Colour: Low angle medium close-up of ANNE, wearing a sheepskin jacket and dark glasses, watching a take on the film set.
462. Sepia: Medium close-up of JEAN-LOUIS in profile, driving in Ford overalls.
463. A high shot, panning with a BMW as it comes fast up a mountain road.
464. Similar shot of a Peugeot going away from camera.
465. Colour: Medium shot of a movie camera on a truck

89

with the DIRECTOR *and the* CAMERAMAN. ANNE *is sitting on the base. Some assistants push the truck along sideways, following the camels as they pass in the foreground.*
466. Sepia: A snow-covered road, glittering in the sunlight. Seen from a following car, an Alfa Romeo speeds past a van, away from camera.
467. Pan with a Cortina in medium shot as it rounds a snow-covered hairpin bend.
468. Colour: Medium close-up of ANNE *looking through the camera view-finder.*
469. Sepia: High angle medium shot of the Mustang coming up a snow-bound road. Pan as it skids round a bend. (Still on page 60)
470 Colour: Resume on ANNE, *still looking through the view-finder. (Still on page 60) She beckons to the* DIRECTOR, *who comes and takes her place.*
471. Sepia: Pan with a Mercedes as it slides rapidly round a snow-covered bend towards camera.
472. Colour: Medium close-up. Without hearing them, we see ANNE *and the* DIRECTOR *in conversation by the camera. The music continues over, then cuts out and we hear the roar of the Mustang's engine.*
473. Close-up of JEAN-LOUIS *in profile, in the passenger seat of the Mustang, glancing down at his route instructions and relaying them to* CHEMIN, *off-screen.*
JEAN-LOUIS : Straight on, then fork left.
474. High angle close-up of the pad of instructions on JEAN-LOUIS' *knee.*
CHEMIN *off* : Yes.
475. Long shot of the Mustang sweeping up a snowy road towards camera with dipped headlamps. (Still on page 61)
JEAN-LOUIS *off* : Straight ahead.
476. Colour: Medium close-up of ANNE *in front of the camels, turning round to address someone off-screen.*
477. Sepia: Medium close-up of JEAN-LOUIS *reading the route instructions out to* CHEMIN, *off-screen. (Still on page 61)*
478. Medium shot, panning with the Mustang as it

90

rounds a left-hand bend.
479. Resume on JEAN-LOUIS, *in profile.*
480. Another panning shot; the Mustang slithers round another bend.
481. Resume on JEAN-LOUIS, *in profile.*
482. Colour: Low angle close-up of ANNE *and the* DIRECTOR *standing in front of the camera in brilliant sunlight, talking. The noise of the car continues over.*
483. Sepia: Medium close-up as the Mustang screeches round a bend towards camera.
484. Colour: Medium close-up of ANNE *and the* DIREC-TOR *discussing a take, script in hand.*
485. Sepia: A high shot of the Mustang moving away from camera.
486. Medium close-up of CHEMIN *driving, three-quarter back view.*
487. Pan left as the car rounds another bend in medium shot.
488. Close-up of JEAN-LOUIS *in profile, glancing at his notes.*
489. A high shot, panning with the Mustang as it comes up a snowy road.
490. Medium close-up of a Mercedes rounding a bend away from camera.
491. Medium close-up of JEAN-LOUIS; *he turns a page of his notes.*
492. Colour: A high shot, panning with ANNE *as she walks about by the camera truck. The theme music comes in again, then fades to be replaced by the sound of the Mustang, and* JEAN-LOUIS' *voice.*
JEAN-LOUIS *off* : Left ahead.
CHEMIN : Okay.
493. Sepia: Medium shot of the Mustang seen from a following car with the windscreen wipers going. The Mustang rounds a bend covered in thick snow, throwing up a shower from its back wheels, skidding and hooting loudly.
494. Colour: High angle medium shot of ANNE *adjusting an* ACTOR'S *costume. A camel moves across the fore-*

ground.

495. Sepia: It is night. A car passes rapidly, hooting, its headlamps lighting up a sign marked CHECKPOINT.

496. High angle medium shot of mechanics working on a damaged car, while the voice of the COMMENTATOR *resumes.*

COMMENTATOR *off:* . . . A large number of cars have now dropped out, in fact out of the 273 starters only 80 are still running. There have been a lot of accidents and the weather has caused a lot of problems; the roads are like an ice-rink. As I said earlier, it's hell. Right now . . .

497–499. As the COMMENTATOR *speaks, three similar high angle shots of mechanics working in the dark at the checkpoint, jacking up a car, rolling wheels, etc. (Still on page 62)*

500. Medium close-up of a competitor's card being quickly inserted in the clocking-in machine at the checkpoint.

501. Pan with a MARSHAL *as he rushes across with the card to a waiting Rover 2000.*

502. Medium shot as a Triumph 2000 halts by a waiting MARSHAL.

503. As 499. The MARSHAL *hands the Triumph driver his card. Pan as the car moves off.*

504. High angle shot as a Volvo DRIVER *receives his card and moves off.*

505. High angle medium close-up of an OFFICIAL *stamping a card in the checkpoint booth.*

506. Medium shot seen through the window of the booth. A COMPETITOR *dashes in.*

507. High angle medium shot. The Mustang stops by the waiting MARSHAL.

508. Medium shot across the car as the MARSHAL *hands back their card and it moves off. Pan right as it accelerates away into the darkness.*

509. Colour: Medium close-up of ANNE, *facing camera, on the platform of a Parisian bus, crossing the Place de la Concorde. (Still on page 62)* **In** *the background we catch a glimpse of the Arc de Triomphe at the other end*

of the Champs Elysées. The bus stops and ANNE *gets off.*
510. Sepia: Low angle medium close-up of JEAN-LOUIS,
facing camera. He is driving in a knitted cardigan, wear-
ing glasses and unshaven. (Still on page 62)
511. High angle medium close-up of CHEMIN *lying*
asleep across the back seat. (Still on page 62)
512. Medium close-up of CHEMIN *driving, in profile;*
pan to show JEAN-LOUIS *asleep in the back.*
513. Colour: Medium close-up of a greengrocer's display
in a street in Paris. ANNE *comes into frame and is served*
by a WOMAN *in the foreground, while we hear the sound*
of a car skidding round a bend, off.
CHEMIN *off* : Right hairpin. . . .
JEAN-LOUIS *off* : Yes.
514. Sepia: Medium close-up of JEAN-LOUIS *in profile,*
driving.
515. Colour: A blurred image of ANNE *in medium close-*
up, surrounded by flowers.
CHEMIN *off* : Left hairpin.
JEAN-LOUIS *off* : Yes.
Scream of tyres and sound of the Mustang's horn, off.
516. Sepia: Shot of a road at night. Pan right as a
car passes, skidding, headlamps ablaze. Sparks fly as its
studded tyres dig into the road.*
517. Colour: Long shot up the Champs Elysées with the
Arc de Triomphe in the background. ANNE *walks towards*
us in the middle of the road, looking for a taxi. (Still
on page 62) We hear the beginning of one of PIERRE'S
songs. Camera pans as ANNE *finally spots a free taxi and*
runs across the road between the cars.
518. Medium close-up of her, the collar of her sheepskin
coat drawn up round her ears. Zoom back to show her
sitting on a bench in the avenue near the Place de la
Concorde, dreaming.
The song is sung by NICOLE CROISILLE.
SONG *off* : ' Once
We lived in the town, you and I.

---

* End of the seventh reel, 410 metres.

For a long time our hearts
Through the streets would range.
Amongst many a glance
Which would cross and pass by,
Yours and mine by chance
Ceased to be strange.
It's you today,
It's me today,
Today love has taken us by the arm.
And if it all goes too fast, too bad,
Since love invites us to be glad,
And to live wholeheartedly
What the future has in store.
It's you today,
It's me today,
Today love has taken us by the arm.
And if it all goes too fast, too bad,
Since love invites us to be glad,
And to live wholeheartedly
What the future has in store.'

The series of alternating shots continues throughout the song.
519. Sepia: Medium close-up of JEAN-LOUIS chatting to CHEMIN while a jerrycan is emptied into the Mustang's tank in the foreground.
520. Colour: Close-up of ANNE, lost in thought, her sheepskin collar pressed to her cheek.
521. Sepia: High angle medium shot: the Mustang, its headlamps on, loses control on a snow-covered bend and spins right round in a circle before starting off again.
522. A closer shot as it moves off.
523. Long shot, tracking out in front of the Mustang as it comes out of the bend, swerving wildly.
524. A closer tracking shot of the car, headlamps ablaze.
525. Medium close-up of JEAN-LOUIS' hands on the wheel.
526. Colour: Close-up of ANNE lost in thought. She smiles to herself.

94

527. Sepia: Close-up of JEAN-LOUIS *in profile, wearing a crash-helmet as he drives. He answers* CHEMIN'S *route instructions, his voice covered by the song.*

528. Colour: Medium shot tracking with ANNE, *in the Jardin des Tuileries, walking by a pool with a swan moving slowly across it.*

529. Sepia: Pan with the Mustang as it slithers round an icy bend.

530. Close-up of JEAN-LOUIS *from behind as he sits in the passenger seat, navigating.*

531. Pan with the car in high angle long shot as it moves along a road in the middle of a wide expanse of snow.

532. Medium close-up of JEAN-LOUIS *in profile, navigating.*

533. Close-up of him, also in profile. (Still on page 63)

534. Colour: Medium close-up of ANNE, *facing camera, sitting in the hairdresser's under a dryer. She is reading, apparently with great interest, a magazine called ' Moteurs '. (Still on page 63)*

535. Sepia: A checkpoint in the snow: loud noise of cars passing. A dazzling pair of headlamps comes towards camera.

536. Pan right round with a Citroen as it screams through the checkpoint and off up the snowy road.

537–538. Two more panning shots; a Cortina, then another Citroen pass at incredible speed, throwing up snow at the side of the narrow road.

539. Pan with another car as it races past a warning sign saying ' ICE '.

540. Wide shot of the finish at Monte Carlo, in sunlight, still in sepia, with an expectant crowd. As the COMMEN-TATOR *speaks, off, we see a succession of brief shots.*

COMMENTATOR *off* : Well, it's now a quarter of an hour since the last competitor arrived, the forty-second to be precise, since only forty-two cars finally made it to Monte Carlo. . . .

541. Close-up of a COMPETITOR *talking through his car window.*

542. Medium close-up of JEAN-LOUIS *in the Mustang, talking to a* RADIO COMMENTATOR *with a microphone.*

(Still on page 63)

543. A slightly closer shot of the same. Their voices are covered by that of the COMMENTATOR.

544. Reverse shot through the car window, CHEMIN *in the foreground with an unlit cigarette in his mouth,* JEAN-LOUIS *and the* INTERVIEWER *in the background.*

COMMENTATOR *off* : That will give you some idea of the difficulties encountered in this competition, which has been as gruelling for the mechanics as for the drivers. Monte Carlo, as you know, is the capital of gambling . . . well, tonight Monte Carlo will be the capital of motoring.

545. Medium close-up of a DRIVER *kissing his wife.*

546. A longer shot of the same. We see that the car has lost its windscreen and the DRIVER *is leaning out through the front.*

547–550. Four similar close-ups of JEAN-LOUIS *and his fellow drivers in the Ford team discussing the rally.*

551. High angle medium close-up of JEAN-LOUIS *driving off in the Mustang as the* COMMENTATOR *continues.*

COMMENTATOR *off* : We would have liked to be able to show you pictures of Prince Rainier and Princess Grace, but unfortunately they were not here for the finish as they are at present away skiing . . .

552. Medium shot of a crowd of photographers and cameramen photographing the presentation of the trophies off-screen.

553–554. Two similar medium shots of the winners being presented with their trophies.

COMMENTATOR *off* : . . . and so they were unable to present the trophies to the winners, who are not the real winners since as you know it is Makinen and the other Cooper drivers who should have won . . .

555. Black and white, blue filter. Wide shot of ANNE'S *apartment with a television set in the middle of the picture.* ANNE *is out of focus, in back view in the foreground, while on the television screen facing us we see a news programme covering the finish at Monte Carlo.*

COMMENTATOR *continuing from the television set* : . . . but they were disqualified over a small detail in the regulations. A regrettable occurrence, as I am sure you will agree . . . but no doubt it will all be forgotten this evening at the dance to which all the competitors have been invited, at the Sporting Club which is . . .

556. The COMMENTATOR'S *voice cuts out. Reverse angle medium close-up of* ANNE, *facing camera, sitting in an armchair, smoking. She has just picked up the telephone. (Still on page 63) Soft music.*

ANNE : Hello, I would like to send a telegram to Monte Carlo. *A pause.* Yes, thank you. *A pause.* Hello, yes, to Monte Carlo. Monsieur Jean-Louis Duroc . . . Duroc with a C. *A pause.* Well, that's the problem, I don't know the address . . . yes I'm sorry, but it's quite easy, he's a driver . . . in the Monte Carlo Rally. Oh yes, if you'd be so kind. *A pause.* Yes, that's it. No, the Sporting Club will do fine, yes. Right, er . . . *Hesitating.* ' Bravo, I saw you on the television. Anne.' No, no, wait . . . ' Bravo, I love you. Anne.' Yes, that's it, yes. Montmartre 15-40 . . . Mademoiselle . . .

557. An aerial view of the bay of Monte Carlo at night, all lit up. Black and white through a blue filter.

ANNE *continues, off* : . . . How soon will it get there? *A pause.* Thank you.

558. Loud music. Interior shot of the ballroom at the Sporting Club in Monte Carlo, at night. The whole of this scene is shot in black and white with a blue filter. In the foreground, couples in evening dress are seated at tables. A troupe of girls are dancing on the stage.
559. Medium shot of the girls dancing on stage, waving long sashes.
560. High angle long shot of the stage. Camera pans across the ballroom to show couples dancing on the floor, and more people seated in the gallery above.
561. Pan to follow a WAITER *in high angle medium long shot, as he makes his way through the dancers towards the table where* JEAN-LOUIS *and* HENRI CHEMIN *are sitting with a mixed party of friends, all in evening dress. The* WAITER *holds out a tray to* JEAN-LOUIS, *bearing a*

telegram. JEAN-LOUIS *opens it and then exchanges a few words with* CHEMIN *who is sitting next to him. He rises and takes leave of his companions, putting the telegram in his pocket as he goes. Pan to follow* JEAN-LOUIS *making his way quickly to the door.*
562. *Medium shot, tracking after* JEAN-LOUIS *as he hurries towards the reception desk in the vestibule. He asks for his bill and runs back towards camera, taking off his dinner jacket. (Still on page 63) Pan to follow him in back view as he rushes down the corridor leading to the bedrooms.*

563. *Long shot of a B.P. service station at night; black and white with blue filter. A pair of headlights appear in the distance. Camera pans as a white Mustang, covered in dirt, screeches to a halt by the pumps.**
564. *High angle medium close-up of* JEAN-LOUIS *as he gets out and, seeing no one around, presses the horn impatiently. Camera pans and tracks after him as he walks towards the lighted office. Noise of cars passing on the road.* JEAN-LOUIS *tries to open the door of the office, which is locked. We can see the pump* ATTENDANT *asleep inside. Track in further as* JEAN-LOUIS *knocks on the door. (Still on page 64) The* ATTENDANT *wakes up and stares at* JEAN-LOUIS *for several seconds before registering that he has a customer. Taking his time, he removes the rug covering his legs, puts on his cap, gets up and opens the door. As he comes out he hunches his shoulders against the cold.*
JEAN-LOUIS : Good evening. I'm sorry to bring you out in this cold.
Camera pans as they walk towards the car.
ATTENDANT : Bit nippy, isn't it? Not exactly mild these last few weeks. . . . Super or regular?
JEAN-LOUIS : Super. . . .
The ATTENDANT *stands interrogatively by the pump.*

---

* The car used in this shot, and from now to the end of the film, bears the number 184, and would therefore appear to be a different one from that which JEAN-LOUIS drove in the rally.

JEAN-LOUIS *puts on his coat, which he has just taken out of the car.*

JEAN-LOUIS : Can you fill her up?

ATTENDANT : Fill her up?

JEAN-LOUIS : Yes.

ATTENDANT : Well, it's a bit of a bother filling her up, 'cause it never comes out a round figure. . . . Then it's nothing but small change and you see we have to add it all up in the morning. . . . You can imagine what it's like for us adding up all that small change. . . .

JEAN-LOUIS : Okay, give me fifty francs' worth.

The ATTENDANT *brings the nozzle across to the Mustang.* JEAN-LOUIS *stands near by, watching and smoking a cigarette. The* ATTENDANT *pauses and looks fixedly at* JEAN-LOUIS. *(Still on page 64)*

JEAN-LOUS *indicating the petrol cap* : You have to turn it.

ATTENDANT : Yes, but . . . er . . . the cigarette.

JEAN-LOUIS *grinding it out with his foot* : There.

Pan with JEAN-LOUIS *as he walks round the car, absent-mindedly kicking the tyres. We hear him talking to himself as he does so. Then he comes back towards the* ATTENDANT.

JEAN-LOUIS, *interior monologue* : It's quite something to send a telegram like that . . . you've got to have guts. . . . No, really, it's extraordinary for a beautiful woman . . . to send a telegram like that — it's marvellous! I'd never have done a thing like that. It's fantastic coming from a woman, fantastic. What guts.*

565. *We are on the road again, at night; blue filter. Medium close-up of* JEAN-LOUIS *facing camera through the windscreen. It is pouring with rain and the wipers are in action.*

JEAN-LOUIS, *interior monologue* : If I keep up this average I shall be in Paris around . . . six o'clock, half past six. *A pause.* Six, half past six, she'll almost certainly be asleep. What shall I do? I'll go into a café, telephone her from there. She'll be at home. . . . If a woman sends you a telegram saying ' I

---

* End of the eighth reel, 300 metres.

love you ' . . . *Zoom in closer.* . . . you can arrive without asking. After all, what am I going there for? Anyway, I go to her place . . . I don't know what floor she lives on, so I have to wake the concierge . . . and then the concierge will say : ' She's not there ', or perhaps : ' You can't go up at this hour.' I'll say to her : ' I'm sorry, but I've just driven five thousand kilometres . . .' *He grins.* . . . six thousand . . . it's six thousand with the return journey. ' I've just driven six thousand kilometres to see Madame Gauthier. I'm sorry but I'm going up.' I go up, ring once, twice. No, I'll ring once. No point in alarming her. *A car passes, out of frame. Noise and effect of headlamps.* I ring once. She's some time coming. . . . Perhaps she doesn't open the door, but says : ' Who is it?' Then I say . . . um, I say . . . ' It's Jean-Louis, Antoine's father.' Oh no, I can't say that. I'll say : ' It's Antoine's father.' Yes, that'll sound good. *Zoom back to show him in medium close-up as at the beginning of the shot.* ' Who is it?' — ' Antoine's father.' So . . . *Sound of another car passing.* . . . she opens the door and there we are, face to face. *Zoom in again. A pause.* She'll be embarrassed, of course, sending me a telegram like that, saying : ' I love you.' *Noise of a car passing.* . . . Yes, she'll be embarrassed, it's quite natural. . . . *Zoom back.* She's there . . . and she's embarrassed. So she says : ' I'll make some coffee.' That's it. *Resuming his train of thought, looking pleased with himself.* ' You've come a long way. I'll make you some coffee.' So I go in. *Zoom forward.* No, I must say something myself, after all. I'm hopeless, what a coward. . . . So I'll say to her. . . . I ought to stop in Avignon and send her a telegram. Yes, that's a good idea. Oh, no, no. . . . Supposing she's woken up by the telephone at a quarter to six . . . I'll look a bit stupid arriving at six. No, she'll have gone to sleep in the meantime . . . *Zoom back again.* . . . and she won't be at all pleased at being woken up again. . . . No, that's a stupid idea. Anyway, fortunately I've . . . *We hear the first few notes of the theme music.* . . . I've got quite a way to go, plenty of time to think of something. *Music.*

566. *Normal colour. Long shot through the windscreen as the Mustang travels along a main road bordered with*

trees. It is very early morning, the overall colour is still blue, and the sky is dull and overcast. In front of us, moving away from the camera, a Citroen DS passes another car at high speed. Its left indicator flashes as it moves out, a single spot of yellow in the blue picture. Then the Mustang overtakes the Citroen.

567. Medium close-up of JEAN-LOUIS *in profile. He takes an electric shaver from the dashboard and starts to shave as he drives. (Still on page 64) Outside the sky lightens as the sun begins to rise. The music gets louder.*

568. Medium close-up of JEAN-LOUIS' *hand on the steering wheel.*

569. Resume on JEAN-LOUIS *shaving. Tilt down as, still holding the razor, he changes gear.*

570. Medium shot looking out of the car window. A road sign bearing the words ' PARIS MELUN ETAMPES *' flashes past.*

571. Sideways tracking shot of the countryside, seen through the window of the car, the rising sun appearing intermittently between the silhouettes of houses and trees. The music continues with a choir singing.

572. High angle medium shot, panning with the car as it comes and stops outside number 14, rue Lamarck. Tilt up as JEAN-LOUIS *leaps out, rings at the door and goes in. Zoom in through the entrance hall as he goes and knocks on the glazed door of the* CONCIERGE'S *quarters.*

JEAN-LOUIS *at the door* : Anne Gauthier, please.

CONCIERGE *sleepily, off* : Second floor, on the left.

JEAN-LOUIS : Thank you.

He runs up the stairs, and out of frame. The camera tilts up and across the façade of the building to show an unlighted window on the second floor, then tilts down again to show the CONCIERGE'S *door at the end of the hall.* JEAN-LOUIS *appears and knocks again.*

JEAN-LOUIS : I'm sorry . . . there's no one there.

CONCIERGE *off* : Well, she doesn't always tell me what she's doing.

JEAN-LOUIS *comes away looking disappointed. He lights a cigarette, then comes to a decision. He goes back and,*

*straightening up and puffing out his chest, knocks again
on the door. (Still on page 64)*
JEAN-LOUIS *loudly* : Police!
CONCIERGE *off* : I think she's gone to see her little girl in
Deauville.
JEAN-LOUIS : Thank you.
*Zoom back as he runs out, leaps back into the car and
drives off. The choir continues to sing.*
*573. High angle long shot of the countryside in daylight.
Camera pans with the white Mustang as* JEAN-LOUIS
*sweeps round a long curve at high speed, changes down
and roars off to the right.*
*574. Medium shot of the entrance to the school in
Deauville. The door opens and the* HEADMISTRESS *comes
out followed by* JEAN-LOUIS.
HEADMISTRESS : I was surprised to see you arriving here. I
saw you on the television yesterday, in the Monte Carlo Rally.
It was very good.
Tilt down as they come down the steps.
JEAN-LOUIS : So you think I might find them down there? *He
goes out of frame.*
HEADMISTRESS : Oh yes. I'm sure you will. You know where
it is, past the landing stage?
JEAN-LOUIS *crossing to the car at bottom of frame* : Past . . .
Oh, yes . . . er, if they come back while I'm gone, can you
tell them to wait? *(Production still on page 64)*
HEADMISTRESS : Yes, of course.
JEAN-LOUIS : Goodbye.
HEADMISTRESS : Goodbye. See you shortly.
*Zoom back as the Mustang turns in the driveway and
moves off. Zoom forward again to show the* HEAD-
MISTRESS *going slowly up the steps to the door.*

*There follows a series of exterior shots of Deauville. It is
a misty day; the sky is overcast and the sea grey-green.
The scene is shot in normal colour, but the overall effect
is deliberately dull.*
575. Medium close-up of JEAN-LOUIS *driving the white
Mustang bearing the number 184. He looks from side to*

side. *(Still on page 81)*

576. *Medium shot, tracking sideways with the Mustang as* JEAN-LOUIS *drives along by the harbour wall, his arm hanging out of the window. A boat's siren sounds, off.*

577. *Medium close-up of the car, then zoom back as it turns and takes a road leading to the beach.*

578. *Medium close-up of* JEAN-LOUIS, *back to camera, standing with his hands in his pockets on the wooden jetty which overlooks the beach. He searches the horizon then turns to face camera, and his eye falls on something off-screen. Music.*

579. *Long shot: camera tracks sideways as he runs along the jetty to his car, which is parked just beneath the lighthouse. Hold as he jumps into it, then pan as he drives back along the jetty, towards the beach.*

580. *Medium close-up, tracking sideways with the car. Zoom back as it bumps across the promenade and speeds along, intermittently obscured by the promenade shelters.*

581. *Low angle long shot, tracking with the car as it moves along in front of the colonnaded promenade, the beach in the foreground.* ANNE *and the two children appear, playing on the beach, as the Mustang turns and stops some distance behind them. They do not notice it.* JEAN-LOUIS *gets out and flashes the headlamps.*

582. *Low angle medium close-up of the front of the car, headlamps flashing wildly. (Still on page 81)*

583. *Resume on long shot, the car in the background with its lights still on.* ANNE *and the children turn and run towards it as* JEAN-LOUIS *dashes down the beach towards them. The choir sings the theme music.* ANNE *and* JEAN-LOUIS *run into each other's arms. He lifts her and whirls her round, hugging her close, while the children gambol happily around them. (Still on page 81)*

584. *Medium close-up, panning with* JEAN-LOUIS *as he dances round in a circle, whirling* ANNE *in his arms.*

585. *High angle medium shot of a dog playing on the beach: camera pans to and fro as he trots up to the water's edge and then, frightened by the waves, runs back to his master, who is strolling along, using a piece*

of driftwood as a walking-stick. (Still on page 81)*

586. Medium close-up of the car outside the school. In the background the HEADMISTRESS *and the two children are standing on the steps, waving goodbye.*

HEADMISTRESS : Well . . . see you next Sunday.

ANTOINE *and* FRANÇOISE : Goodbye, daddy! Goodbye, mummy!

The car starts to move off.

587. High angle medium close-up of the car from the front as it moves off.

588. Resume on the HEADMISTRESS *and the two children, still waving happily. (Still on page 81) Zoom forwards as the* HEADMISTRESS *ushers the children in through the door.*

589. Long shot of the beach with the dog still playing on the sands, lit by the rays of the setting sun. Camera follows it as it gambols round its master, running up to the water's edge and then running away as the waves come in. The music ends.

During the following sequence, which takes place in a hotel bedroom, we see a series of alternating shots, first of ANNE *and* JEAN-LOUIS *in bed, shot in colour through a deep orange filter, then of* ANNE'S *reminiscences of her life with* PIERRE, *shot in normal colour. The sequence is accompanied by the song ' In the shadow we leave ', by* PIERRE BAROUH.

590. Before the song starts there is a long silence, during which we see ANNE *lying naked in bed, shot in close-up through the orange filter.* JEAN-LOUIS' *hands tenderly stroke her hair and cheek. He comes into frame, naked, back to camera; they kiss passionately.*

591. Close-up of JEAN-LOUIS, *back to camera, lying on top of* ANNE.

592. Close-up from the side. JEAN-LOUIS *runs his hands through her hair. (Still on page 82)*

593. Close-up of her hand on the back of his neck.

---

* End of the ninth reel, 245 metres.

594. *High angle close-up. They kiss.*
595. *Tilt down as she runs her hand, wearing her wedding ring, down his arm.*
596. JEAN-LOUIS *on top of* ANNE. *Sighs of pleasure.*
597. ANNE *on top of* JEAN-LOUIS, *her hand on his.*
598. *A similar shot. He gently strokes her throat. She lays her hand over his.*
599. JEAN-LOUIS *on top of* ANNE.
600. *Close-up of their hands, clasping each other tight on the pillow.*
601. *A sigh, as he moves on top of her again.*
602. *She lies on his chest; her hair almost fills the screen.*
603. *The two of them kissing,* ANNE *with the sheet drawn up over her.*
604. *Another sigh, as he moves, lying on top of her.*
605. *Extreme close-up, her face on the pillow, his head above hers.*
606. *The two of them from the side, her hands on his back.*
607. *Close-up of* ANNE *from above, facing camera, and* JEAN-LOUIS, *back to camera, on top of her.* ANNE'S *pleasure seems to fade; her eyes open for a moment as we hear an amplified heartbeat, off. She listens, screwing up her eyes. The picture blurs, and the song begins, accompanied by an organ and by the sound of the heartbeat.**

PIERRE'S SONG *off* :
' In the shadow we leave
There will always remain
Always in love's name
A taste of eternity.
In the name of our love
A shadow will remain.
This shadow of ours,

---

* For convenience, the text of the song is given first, followed by the accompanying shots, each one of which corresponds approximately to one line of the song. All the shots of ANNE and JEAN-LOUIS are taken through the orange filter, all those of ANNE and PIERRE in normal colour. They are all very short.

How many suns
Burning the sky
Have had to combine
That from all these suns
A shadow will remain.
These suns . . . they are so warm, they are so fierce
That they burn us, and our hearts they pierce
Again, and again, and again.
Their names are mere clichés :
Love, respect, and madness.
Confidence and courage too,
The purest picture-book blue :
All that you expect from me,
All I expect you to be.
Ah me ! Ah me !
In the shadow we leave
Nothing will bloom
In the days to come,
Nothing except for beauty.
Even in the depth of gloom
A shadow will remain,
The shadow we leave.
By the thousand suns
Of another love
Nothing can be changed.
For from these first suns
A shadow will remain.
These suns . . . They are so warm, they are so fierce
That they burn us, and our hearts they pierce
Again, and again, and again.
One can only smile at their names
There's passion and also delirium sometimes
Then there's panache and tenderness too
And from our youth the purest blue :
All the things that will outlive me,
All the things that forever will be,
In the shadow we leave. . . .'
Corresponding shots:
608. High angle close-up of ANNE *and* PIERRE *rolling in*

the snow and kissing.

609. JEAN-LOUIS, on top of ANNE, kisses her as she closes her eyes with an expression of pain.

610. Medium close-up of PIERRE and ANNE lying in the snow, laughing and kissing.

611. JEAN-LOUIS caresses ANNE's neck, while she gazes fixedly upwards.

612. PIERRE and ANNE in the snow, entwined in each other's arms.

613. JEAN-LOUIS on top of ANNE. She drops her head on the pillow, looking anguished.

614. PIERRE rolls away from ANNE in the snow; she rolls over onto him, laughing. (Still on page 82)

615. As 613. JEAN-LOUIS caresses her face and presses her to him. (Still on page 83)

616. ANNE and PIERRE roll over and over down a snowy slope, entwined in each other's arms, deep blue sky above them.

617. ANNE, lying beneath JEAN-LOUIS, puts her hand over her eyes and seems to exclaim in anguish.

618. PIERRE and ANNE still rolling down the slope.

619. As 617. JEAN-LOUIS lies motionless on top of her. She turns her head away.

620. A closer shot of ANNE and PIERRE, still rolling crazily down the slope, locked together.

621. ANNE under JEAN-LOUIS; zoom in to extreme close-up of her anguished face.

622. PIERRE and ANNE lie back, gazing up into the sun. She kisses him passionately. (Still on page 83)

623. Extreme close-up of ANNE's eyes, full of sadness and nostalgia.

624. PIERRE and ANNE galloping side by side across the Camargue.

625. Close-up of ANNE's face as she lies under JEAN-LOUIS. She moves her head from side to side.

626. Extreme close-up of PIERRE and ANNE, kissing.

627. ANNE, under JEAN-LOUIS, screws up her eyes with the pain of remembrance.

628. Profile of PIERRE; he mouths ' I love you.' Pan to

107

profile of ANNE; *she does the same.*

629. ANNE, *with* JEAN-LOUIS *on top of her. She closes her eyes and draws a hand across her forehead.*

630. *Medium shot of* ANNE *and* PIERRE *from the side, having a meal on a balcony. She kisses his hand while he talks to her earnestly. (Still on page 83)*

631. *Close-up of their faces,* PIERRE *holding a baby's bottle.*

632. ANNE *feeds the bottle to a lamb, which is held by* PIERRE. *They both laugh.*

633. ANNE *and* PIERRE *stand with their heads out of shot, conversing with a* SHEPHERD *who is holding the lamb hanging by its front legs. The lamb's mother licks it as it hangs, and it kicks. (Still on page 83)*

634. *Medium shot of* PIERRE *and* ANNE, *through a telephoto lens, walking through a flock of sheep. Zoom back.*

635. ANNE *lies under* JEAN-LOUIS, *frowning.*

636. PIERRE *and* ANNE *at a dog kennels with* PIERRE *inside a wire-netting enclosure. Tilt down and zoom back as* PIERRE *crouches down and caresses the dogs; they jump up at him eagerly.*

637. JEAN-LOUIS' *naked back, with* ANNE, *a blurred and distant figure beneath him. She presses a hand to her forehead.*

638. *Back view of* PIERRE *and* ANNE *driving in a convertible with the top down, the camera on the back of the car.* ANNE *has her arm around her husband and kisses him as he drives. Another car overtakes them.*

639. ANNE *lying under* JEAN-LOUIS. *She frowns and lets out an exclamation.*

640. ANNE *and* PIERRE, *their heads close together,* ANNE *wearing a peaked cap.*

641. *Camera pulls focus to show* ANNE, *in extreme close-up, moving restlessly under* JEAN-LOUIS.

642. *Profile of* PIERRE, *his head leant against a tree trunk. Pan right to show* ANNE *doing likewise, gazing across at him, the wind blowing the fur collar of her coat.*

643. *Medium shot of* PIERRE *lying back on a pile of hay,*

ANNE *leaning her head against his raised knee, a vast château in soft focus in the background.*

644. Extreme close-up of PIERRE, *in profile, his head against* ANNE'S *hair as he whispers in her ear. Suddenly she starts back.*

645. Soft focus, extreme close-up of ANNE *under* JEAN-LOUIS. *Camera focuses as she moves her head restlessly, then moves out of focus again.*

646. Very long shot of ANNE *and* PIERRE *standing clasped together, silhouetted against the sky and framed by two towers. Zoom right back to show the towers and battlements of a castle on either side. (Still on page 83)*

647. Medium close-up of ANNE *and* PIERRE *in a cornfield.*

648. Sideways tracking shot as the two of them walk along the quayside in a small Mediterranean port.

649. Close-up of PIERRE *putting on a hat in a market.*

650. PIERRE *putting on a pair of round, horn-rimmed glasses. Pan to* ANNE, *watching with tenderness and amusement.*

651. Orange filter. The words of the song end, and the heartbeat and music get louder. Medium close-up of ANNE'S *head in profile on a pillow, eyes closed, an ecstatic expression on her face. This time it is* PIERRE'S *face which appears over her. (Still on page 84) He kisses her repeatedly with increasing passion. They come to a climax.*

652. Close-up of ANNE'S *head on the pillow, at first out of focus. Finally she opens her eyes; it is* JEAN-LOUIS *who is lying on top of her.*

653. Medium close-up of the two of them lying in bed, in profile. ANNE *appears to murmur, almost imperceptibly:* 'Pierre!' *. . . Then she shuts her eyes.* JEAN-LOUIS *raises himself slightly and looks at her. (Still on page 84)*

JEAN-LOUIS : Why? *After a while* ANNE *opens her eyes.* JEAN-LOUIS *repeats his question, almost desperately* : Why?

ANNE *softly, after a pause* : Because of my husband.

---

* End of the tenth reel, 408 metres.

JEAN-LOUIS : But he's dead.
A long silence follows. She shakes her head.

*654. Long shot of the promenade at Deauville, normal
colour. The scene is bathed in the yellowish rays of the
afternoon sun. The wind is whipping up the waves and
blowing spray off the sea. We hear the instrumental
introduction to the song 'Love is much stronger than
we are'. A car passes and overtakes a* MAN *walking with
his dog — they are the same pair with an identical gait
which* JEAN-LOUIS *and* ANNE *commented on earlier. The*
MAN *and his dog come slowly towards camera. Two men
on bicycles pass on either side of him.*
655. Black and white, yellowish sepia filter. Medium
close-up, from behind, of* JEAN-LOUIS *in the hotel bedroom as he picks up his jacket from a chair. Camera pans
as he walks across the room, putting on the jacket, and
sits down on the bed, with his back to* ANNE, *who is sitting
on the other side of it in a black petticoat. (Still on page
117) She looks sadly at her handbag, takes out a cigarette
and lights it. During the first two lines of the song, he
half turns to look at her and she lowers her eyes.*
SONG, *woman's voice, off***
'With our past as a guide
Surely we don't need to lie.
We need our mistrust no more.
Love is much stronger than we are.'
ANNE *turning towards him* : I'd better take the train. *She goes
out of frame.*
Slight pan left as JEAN-LOUIS *puts on his watch. He
watches* ANNE *as she passes in front of camera, then he
lights a cigarette.*
SONG, *man's voice, off* :
'Whether one hopes or remains resigned

---

* As in several other places in the film, the exact colour of this particular
filter is difficult to establish, since it tends to vary. Here it is clearly
amber to start with, but has turned gradually to sepia by the time the
couple exit from the lift in shot 656.
** The singer is Nicole Croisille. The male part of the duet is, of course,
Pierre Barouh.

Love bends us easily to its designs
And singles us out from afar.
Love is much stronger than we are.'

JEAN-LOUIS *picking up the telephone*: Room 41 . . . I'd like the bill, please . . . and can you tell me the time of the next train to Paris?

Pan left as ANNE *reappears in back view, fully dressed; then as the woman's voice continues, camera follows her into the bathroom, where she stands in front of the mirror. (Still on page 117) She puts her lighted cigarette down on a shelf and does her hair; then camera tracks out as she comes back towards it, smoking, and re-enters the bedroom. She stands facing* JEAN-LOUIS *as he waits for a reply on the telephone.*

SONG, *woman's voice, off*:
' What can I do when you are near to me?
The times are shot through with mystery;
The evening breeze is sweeter by far;
Love is much stronger than we are.'

656. *Medium close-up of the two of them in the lift, face to face, silent.*

SONG, *man's voice, off*:
' Whether we live free in a wilderness
Or in a cage in happiness,
What does it matter — love makes the choice for us
Love is much stronger than we are.'

They emerge from the lift and, as the song continues, JEAN-LOUIS *walks in front of* ANNE *towards the reception desk, pulling on his raincoat as he goes. Camera tracks out in front of them, losing* ANNE *for a moment then resuming on her as* JEAN-LOUIS *goes off to pay the bill. Hold on medium shot of the reception desk,* ANNE *in the foreground.* JEAN-LOUIS *pockets his wallet and comes towards her, and camera pans after them as they go out through the glass door of the hotel to the Mustang, which is standing in the street outside.*

SONG, *woman's voice, off*:
' We thought we could get away with it;
That to love no more we just had to say it.

111

But love singled us out from afar;
Love is much stronger than we are.'
657. Sepia filter. Low angle close-up of the clock in the
entrance to Deauville station, which says 4.15 pm.
658. Long shot down the platform. On the left is a
stationary train. JEAN-LOUIS *and* ANNE *come slowly*
towards camera and stop by the first class carriage. She
climbs up the steps and turns in the doorway of the
carriage to face JEAN-LOUIS, *who has remained on the*
platform. The song continues off.
SONG *off :*
Woman's voice :　' With our past as a guide
Man's voice :　　' We thought we could get away with it
Woman's voice :　' Surely we don't need to lie
Man's voice :　　' That to love no more we just had to
　　　　　　　　　say it
Woman's voice : ' We need our mistrust no more
The two in chorus : ' Love is much stronger than we are.'
The song ends. JEAN-LOUIS *looks sadly up at* ANNE.
(Still on page 118)
JEAN-LOUIS : Is it a through train?
ANNE : No, I have to change at Evreux.
JEAN-LOUIS *taking a step forward and looking up at her*
beseechingly : Anne . . . why did you tell me your husband
was dead?
659. Close-up of ANNE. *She tries to muster a smile, but*
fails. (Still on page 118)
ANNE : He is dead . . . but he still lives for me. *She turns*
away.
660. Long shot of the platform, the back of the train in
the foreground. A RAILWAYMAN *waves to the* DRIVER
and the train departs. JEAN-LOUIS *watches it as it moves*
away from camera, then turns and walks towards us,
talking to himself (Still on page 118)
JEAN-LOUIS, *interior monologue :* Well, that's one weekend
which didn't end up the way it started. It's ridiculous even
so . . . it's . . . it's ridiculous to prevent oneself from being
happy. *A pause.* If we could start again, what else would I
have done, eh? . . . What else could I have done? . . . See

112

her ' as a friend ' for months and months. . . . Anyway, it comes to the same thing — you start by being friends, you end up just friends. *He glances at his watch.*

> *661. Long shot of the front of the station. The white Mustang turns and comes straight towards camera, head-lamps full on although it is still daylight.*

JEAN-LOUIS, *interior monologue* : She sends me a telegram saying ' I love you ' . . . I just don't understand.

> *662. The sepia filter continues to the end of this sequence. Interior shot of the train taking ANNE to Paris. It is dark outside. Camera is in the corridor and shows ANNE sitting in a corner seat by the window. Two men are asleep beside her, nearest camera. (Still on page 118)*

JEAN-LOUIS, *his interior monologue continuing off* : Her husband must have been quite a guy. Perhaps . . . if he'd lived . . . he'd have been an old fool . . . as it is, he'll always be quite a guy. . . .

> *663. Medium close-up of JEAN-LOUIS seen through the rain-swept windscreen of the Mustang, driving fast; head-lamps flash past outside.*

JEAN-LOUIS, *interior monologue* : Anyway, perhaps he wouldn't have been an old fool . . . they might have been really great together . . . *He wipes the windscreen with his hand.* . . . or they might have been a little old couple like one sees at Monte Carlo.

> *664. Close-up of ANNE in the train. Her sadness seems to lift a little as she remembers the scene in the hotel restaurant which evidently preceded the bedroom scene.*

JEAN-LOUIS *off* : Lyons sausage — is that hot?

WAITER *off* : Oh yes, sir.

JEAN-LOUIS *off* : Where is it? . . .

WAITER *off* : In the hors d'oeuvres.

ANNE *off* : I can't see it . . . let me see.

JEAN-LOUIS *off* : Lyons sausage, Milan sausage and . . .

ANNE *off* : Oh yes!

JEAN-LOUIS *off* : Milan — is that cold?

> *665. Flashback: interior shot of the restaurant, in black and white, sepia filter. JEAN-LOUIS and ANNE are seen in profile, facing each other at a table. A WAITER stands*

between them, facing the camera, as he takes their order.
WAITER : Oh yes, sir, always.
ANNE *brightly* : What's escalope of fresh salmon à la maré-
chale? *(Still on page 118)*
WAITER : It's fresh fish imported from Finland.
JEAN-LOUIS *laughs.*
ANNE *to* JEAN-LOUIS : Have you had it before?
JEAN-LOUIS : No.
ANNE : What shall I have?
    666. Close-up of JEAN-LOUIS *through the windscreen of*
    the Mustang. The wipers are going and his face is inter-
    mittently lit by passing headlamps. The conversation in
    the restaurant continues off.
JEAN-LOUIS *off* : I don't know. . . .
ANNE *off* : I'm not hungry.
    667. Medium close-up of ANNE *in the train, smoking.*
JEAN-LOUIS *off* : Would you like a steak?
ANNE *off* : Yes . . . yes, I think that would be better.
JEAN-LOUIS *off* : Châteaubriand? . . . Châteaubriand . . .
er . . . which is the more tender, Châteaubriand or fillet?
    668. Close-up of JEAN-LOUIS *through the windscreen of*
    the Mustang.
WAITER *off* : Châteaubriand. . . .
JEAN-LOUIS *off* : Châteaubriand, then. . . .
    669. Low angle medium close-up of ANNE, *now standing*
    in the corridor of the train, lost in her recollection of the
    scene.
JEAN-LOUIS *off* : Two Châteaubriands . . . grilled.
WAITER *off* : Grilled, yes. Medium or rare?
    670. Resume on the scene in the restaurant, the couple
    sitting face to face in medium shot, the WAITER *standing.*
ANNE : Medium for me.
JEAN-LOUIS : And for me.
WAITER *writing it down* : Both medium.
JEAN-LOUIS *to the* WAITER *after a pause* : Both hot.
    The WAITER *nods at this superfluous order and then*
    remains standing over JEAN-LOUIS *and* ANNE, *who appear*
    to forget about him. The WAITER *looks embarrassed.*
ANNE *to* JEAN-LOUIS : What time did you leave Monte Carlo

yesterday?

JEAN-LOUIS *looking up as he tries to remember*: I left . . . *He is astonished to see the* WAITER *still standing there.*

WAITER *stammering*: W . . . won't you have anything to start with?

JEAN-LOUIS : No.

The WAITER *moves away, looking disappointed.*

ANNE *smiling*: I think he's upset. . . . We didn't order enough. . . .

JEAN-LOUIS : Shall we cheer him up? . . . *He turns round and calls.* . . . Waiter! . . .

WAITER *hurrying back, his pad at the ready*: Yes, sir?

JEAN-LOUIS : Do you have any rooms?

Music. Long zoom back to show the restaurant from outside, looking in through the window.

671. Medium close-up of ANNE, *her cheek pressed against the window of her compartment as the train speeds through the night. (Still on page 119)*

672–703. Series of thirty-two very quick alternating close-ups of JEAN-LOUIS *driving and* ANNE *sitting in the train or standing in the corridor.* ANNE *looks alternately sad and petulant, while* JEAN-LOUIS *begins to look more cheerful. The cutting gets faster and faster as the sequence proceeds.*

704. Resume on close-up of JEAN-LOUIS *through the windscreen of the Mustang, now grinning to himself as he drives. (Still on page 119)*

705. The sepia filter continues to the end of the film. High angle long shot of the Cour de Rome outside the Gare Saint-Lazare in Paris. It is night. Pan left as the Mustang drives up and stops in front of the station. A few snowflakes begin to fall. JEAN-LOUIS *gets out of the car (Still on page 120) and hurries towards camera, which pans right round to show him from behind as he runs up the steps into the station, two at a time. Music and choir singing.*

706. Medium close-up of ANNE *standing in the corridor of the moving train by the door. She turns to look out.*

707. The interior of the Gare Saint-Lazare at night:

long shot down a platform as a train draws in, coming towards camera. In the foreground JEAN-LOUIS *waits with his back to us, smoking. As the train approaches he starts to walk slowly towards it and the camera tracks forward to follow him. The train stops and a crowd of passengers get out, jostling* JEAN-LOUIS *as they hurry towards the exit.* JEAN-LOUIS *continues to walk along the platform, then suddenly stops. We see* ANNE *getting out of the train and coming towards us. She also stops the moment she sees* JEAN-LOUIS. *(Still on page 120) For a couple of seconds they remain facing each other, a few yards apart, while people hurry past without giving the couple a glance. Suddenly they both rush forwards into each other's arms. Zoom in on the two of them, clasped together, then camera tracks right round them in a circle, finally holding on a medium close-up as* JEAN-LOUIS *takes* ANNE'S *face in his hands. The dark background turns to a luminous white and the frame freezes on the two of them as the film ends.**

---

* Eleventh and final reel, 355 metres.